the new muffin

Sea

GW00359581

Cup

½   125

⅓   80

¼   60

PENGUIN BOOKS

PENGUIN BOOKS
Published by the Penguin Group
Penguin Group (NZ), cnr Airborne and Rosedale Roads, Albany,
Auckland 1310, New Zealand
Penguin Books Ltd, 80 Strand, London, WC2R 0RL, England
Penguin Group (USA) Inc., 375 Hudson Street, New York, NY 10014, United States
Penguin Group (Australia), 250 Camberwell Road, Camberwell,
Victoria 3124, Australia
Penguin Books Canada Ltd, 10 Alcorn Avenue, Toronto,
Ontario, Canada M4V 3B2
Penguin Books (South Africa) (Pty) Ltd, 24 Sturdee Avenue, Rosebank,
Johannesburg 2196, South Africa
Penguin Books India (P) Ltd, 11, Community Centre, Panchsheel Park,
New Delhi 110 017, India
Penguin Ireland Ltd, 25 St Stephen's Green, Dublin 2, Ireland
Penguin Books Ltd, Registered Offices: 80 Strand, London, WC2R 0RL, England

First published by Penguin Group (NZ), 2004
1 3 5 7 9 10 8 6 4 2

Copyright © Carolyn Gibson, 2004

The right of Carolyn Gibson to be identified as the author of this work in terms of
section 96 of the Copyright Act 1994 is hereby asserted.

Designed by Mary Egan
Typeset by Egan-Reid Ltd
Food stylist, Victoria Gibson
Printed in Australia by McPherson's Printing Group

ISBN 0 14 301931 7
A catalogue record for this book is available
from the National Library of New Zealand.

www.penguin.co.nz

contents

introduction

I have vivid memories of the first time I ate a muffin. It was in the early 1960s and my mother was busy baking a much talked-about recipe given to her by a friend of a friend who had a friend in America. I watched as she combined the grit-like ingredients and then poured the gluey mixture into cupcake tins. The smell certainly didn't excite me, nor did their appearance when they finally arrived at the table.

We had heard muffins were supposed to be very healthy, which obviously meant you could eat as many as you wanted. I sank my teeth into the muffin – it had a strange taste and left a tingling of soda on my tongue. We buttered them, jammed them, and ate them until our taste-buds became accustomed, but only because they were from the USA and supposedly healthy.

Since then muffins have experienced an evolution in taste, shape, size, and creativeness. Mini muffins, Texas muffins – what next? We are now spoilt for choice, and therein lies the problem for many of us: too much choice.

We need to keep in mind that in most cases it is not a particular food that is healthy or unhealthy, but rather the way we cook it and the amount we eat. Whether an occasional food is higher or lower in fat is not as important as how often we eat it and what other foods we eat with it on a day-to-day basis.

I don't like to see the word 'guilt-free' on food packaging. Food should not be associated with guilt. If I am going to feel guilty I want it to be over something really bad – not because I have eaten a muffin.

I regularly see people who are distressed about their weight, and who say, 'I do not understand why I can't lose weight when I don't eat any butter or other added fats. I only eat low-fat cakes, muffins and potato chips that are 97% reduced fat.'

The key here is not the fat but the PORTIONS – the QUANTITY – and how much you eat on a DAILY basis.

The fat content in these muffins is lower than in many muffin recipes, and several of the recipes have no fat in them at all. However, remember that you don't have to bake a no-fat or low-fat muffin every time – you can enjoy your 'just desserts' on occasion.

You say you can't be trusted with a batch of muffins? Personally, I would never decide to make a batch of chocolate muffins on a day when I was at home alone and bored. I know my limitations.

However, I would make them for a special occasion, for friends coming over, a shared morning tea or a committee supper, and I would freeze any surplus muffins. Doing this is no guarantee that I won't eat them, but it certainly slows me down.

In *The New Muffin* I have created a simple approach to eating and enjoying muffins.

Breakfast kick-starts the day, but so often it is skipped, or eaten on the run. Eating a muffin at work for breakfast doesn't have to look like you slept in or you are eating breakfast in the company's time. Make a batch of breakfast muffins, freeze some, and then it is just a simple matter of pulling one from the freezer. A quick zap in the microwave at work, a cup of tea or coffee, and you have breakfast. Surprise your family with breakfast muffins as a weekend treat. Let them wake to the aroma of home baking. Our sense of smell can evoke old memories. The wonderful smell of freshly baked muffins could be one of those memories.

For **lunch**, I select one of the savoury muffins I have marked with the letter L which means it contains sufficient protein to make it a meal in itself. I can also add to these savoury muffins a hot vegetable soup on a cold winter's day, a chilled soup in summer, or a crispy mixed green salad. I would never eat a fruit muffin for lunch as although I may feel satisfied at midday, by two o'clock I would be hungry again.

For morning or afternoon **snacks**, you can select either a **sweet** muffin or one of the savoury muffins marked with an S for a snack. These savoury muffins can also be used on the side with soups and salads that contain a protein, such as lentil soup or a chicken salad.

I love **puddings,** and for a treat at the weekends I often have one of my 'just desserts' or special occasion muffins.

My **home-made** jams, conserve, lemon curd and special butters will enhance the taste and enjoyment of eating muffins.

There is something incredibly satisfying about making jam from fruit freshly picked from trees or vines. Make strawberry conserve in summer while fruit is plentiful, and tomato chutney and relish while the vines are groaning under another bumper crop. Dried apricots make delicious jam when fresh fruits are scarce, and in winter when people are begging you to unburden their grapefruit trees you could make my favourite marmalade. Come and visit me at my website at <u>www.carolyngibson.com</u> for more recipes and updates.

I have had lots of fun creating these muffin recipes and although I wanted to bring you lots of variety I have also endeavoured to keep to the KISS principles of Keeping it Simple.

I can't close without extending a huge thank you to my family and friends who shared their ideas and recipes with me, and to my Mum, Gill and Victoria who bravely cooked hundreds of muffins in our test kitchen and who never flinched when I asked them to taste test yet another muffin.

Carolyn

mixing it with the best

There was a time when I had a casual attitude towards baking. It was a case of throw it together, mix it like crazy and hope for the best. My muffins reflected my method – unpredictable and often inedible.

I have now learned that a cup of flour does not mean a cup overflowing above the rim, and a teaspoon should be a level one. Also, preheating the oven and the position of the rack does make a difference to the cooking, and I have mellowed in my desire to beat the life out of the mixture.

Baking muffins is my sort of cooking. There is not a lot of skill required and no special equipment needed. They are made with basic ingredients readily found in an average kitchen, and I don't have to cream the butter and sugar.

Follow my simple rules for making muffins and in no time at all you will be whipping up batches of delicious muffins to delight family and friends.

Successful muffin baking tips

DON'T OVERBEAT YOUR MIXTURE!
It definitely does make a difference. A light hand will produce a lighter muffin. As a guideline for myself, I aim to combine the mixture in less than ten folds of the batter.

MEASURING
All ingredients in my recipes are in metric measures, so use accurate metric measuring cups and spoons. When measuring flour or dry ingredients, spoon them into the measuring cup and level off with a knife. Scooping it into the cup can create an air pocket which may mean not getting an exact measurement. On the other hand, don't tap the flour down in the measuring cup as this in turn will add more of your ingredient.

PRECHECK
Read the recipe and make sure you have all the necessary ingredients on hand before you begin baking.

THE TINS
Grease the muffin tins before you begin mixing. Light rather than heavy greasing is better. If the tins are heavily greased on the sides, it may cause the mixture to 'slip'. Even non-stick tins need to be greased.

I prefer to grease the tins with butter, but you can spray or grease them with oil. I use butter because I find some types of oil have a tendency to burn onto the tin, or not wash off easily.

One of the keys to healthy eating is portion control. Apparently the portions of some foods have increased by 200 per cent. Muffins definitely fall into that category so I am going to suggest you don't use the Texas muffin tins. Over-large muffins are quite daunting to eat, and are often dry and crumbly.

I have used the standard- or mini-muffin-sized tins. Most of my recipes will make twelve standard-sized muffins but if you want a different size it is not necessary to change the recipe. Allow 2–3 minutes less cooking time for mini muffins and 2–4 minutes more for Texas size. Always test muffins are cooked before removing from the oven.

If the recipe is for six muffins, or if you are making half a batch, fill the six empty muffin tins with water to prevent the tray from buckling. Be careful you don't splash your hand with boiling water when removing the tray from the oven.

THE OVEN
Always preheat the oven, and make sure it is at the required temperature before putting the muffins in the oven. You know your own oven best so adjust the recommended temperature if necessary. Place the muffin tray on a rack in the middle of the oven.

THE INGREDIENTS
Baking soda has an alkaline component and needs to be teamed with acidic ingredients. Baking powder on the other hand is both alkaline and acidic. As a general rule I use baking soda (bicarbonate of soda)

when the muffin recipe includes buttermilk or yoghurt, citrus fruits, fresh fruit, honey or maple syrup.

Butter
My personal preference is to cook with butter rather than margarine but you can make your own decision on this. Make sure you allow melted butter to cool before adding to the egg mixture as you don't want to create scrambled eggs. If you want to substitute oil for butter use $1/4$ cup of oil to 60 grams butter.

Buttermilk
If you don't have buttermilk, you can sour milk by adding approximately 1 teaspoon of either vinegar or lemon juice to 1 cup of milk. Leave to stand for a couple of minutes to sour before using.

Eggs
In all the recipes I have used a large (number 7) size egg.

Flour
I suggest using standard flour if the muffin recipe has few ingredients and high-grade flour if the muffin recipe has several heavy ingredients, such as fruits, sausage, wine gums, etc.

Sugar
I have used white sugar unless otherwise stated.

GENERAL TIPS

◆ Allow muffins to cool in tin for 5 minutes – they are easier to remove.

◆ Do not overfill the muffin tin – about three-quarters full is a good guideline.

◆ Always combine dry ingredients well before adding liquid ingredients.

◆ Muffins freeze well and can be reheated when thawed.

muffins for breakfast

nature's harvest of berries, nuts and zesty fruits muffins

2 cups flour
2 teaspoons baking powder
$^1/_2$ teaspoon baking soda
1 teaspoon ground cardamom
1 teaspoon ground ginger
pinch of salt
$^1/_4$ cup soft brown sugar, tightly packed
60 grams butter
$^1/_4$ cup maple syrup
2 eggs
$^2/_3$ cup milk
1 cup mixed frozen berries, slightly thawed
$^1/_2$ cup raisins
12 dried apricots, chopped
12 Brazil nuts, chopped
1 tablespoon grated orange zest

1. Preheat oven to 200°C. Lightly grease 12 muffin tins.
2. Sift together flour, baking powder, baking soda, ground cardamom, ginger and salt into a bowl. Stir in sugar and make a well in the centre.
3. In a pot gently heat the butter and maple syrup. Remove from heat and allow to cool slightly.
4. In another bowl lightly whisk together the eggs and milk. Add the melted butter and maple syrup and stir in mixed berries, raisins, apricots, Brazil nuts and orange zest.
5. Fold fruit mixture into dry ingredients and stir quickly to combine.
6. Spoon mixture into prepared muffin tins and bake for 12–15 minutes or until muffins are golden and spring back when lightly pressed.

Makes 12

grains, dates and cranberry muffins

I like to break these muffins open, drizzle with fruit yoghurt and then eat them with a cake fork.

1¼ cups cranberry juice
½ cup sultanas
1 cup dates, chopped
½ cup rolled oats
½ teaspoon baking soda
1½ cups wholemeal flour
3 teaspoons baking powder
pinch of salt
3 tablespoons sugar
1 teaspoon cinnamon
1 teaspoon mixed spice

1. Preheat oven to 200°C. Lightly grease 12 muffin tins.
2. In a pot combine the cranberry juice, sultanas and dates. Bring to the boil, remove from heat and stir in rolled oats and baking soda. Allow to cool.
3. Sift together flour, baking powder and salt into a bowl. Stir in sugar, cinnamon and mixed spice.
4. Make a well in the centre of the dry ingredients, add the cooled fruit mixture and stir quickly to combine.
5. Spoon mixture into prepared muffin tins and bake for 12–15 minutes or until muffins spring back when lightly pressed.

Makes 12

vanilla buttermilk muffins drizzled with buttery maple syrup

2 cups flour
3 teaspoons baking powder
1 teaspoon baking soda
$1/2$ cup sugar or vanilla sugar (refer page155)
1 teaspoon vanilla essence
40 grams butter, melted
1 cup buttermilk
2 eggs

buttery maple syrup
20 grams butter
2 tablespoons maple syrup

1. Preheat oven to 200°C. Lightly grease 12 muffin tins.
2. Sift together flour, baking powder and baking soda into a bowl. Stir in sugar and make a well in the centre.
3. In another bowl lightly whisk together the vanilla essence, melted butter, buttermilk and eggs.
4. Fold egg mixture into dry ingredients and stir quickly to combine.
5. Spoon mixture into prepared muffin tins and bake for 12–15 minutes or until muffins spring back when lightly pressed.
6. To make buttery maple syrup, melt together butter and maple syrup in a small pot.
7. Serve muffins warm, drizzled with buttery maple syrup and with fresh seasonal fruit on the side.

Makes 12

sweet blueberry and banana muffins

2 tablespoons butter
4 tablespoons liquid honey
2 cups flour
4 teaspoons baking powder
1 teaspoon cinnamon
1 cup cereal bran flakes
$1/4$ cup sugar
1 egg
$3/4$ cup milk
1 banana, chopped
$1^1/2$ cups blueberries

1. Preheat oven to 200°C. Lightly grease 12 muffin tins.
2. In a small pot melt together the butter and honey.
3. Sift together flour, baking powder and cinnamon into a bowl.
4. Stir in the bran flakes and sugar and make a well in the centre.
5. In another bowl lightly whisk together the egg and milk, then add the banana and blueberries.
6. Fold into dry ingredients and stir quickly to combine.
7. Spoon mixture into prepared muffin tins and bake for 12–15 minutes or until muffins spring back when lightly pressed.

Makes 12

honeyed fig and apricot muffins

2 cups flour
2 teaspoons baking powder
$^1/_2$ teaspoon baking soda
1 teaspoon cinnamon
$^1/_2$ cup sugar
pinch of salt
8 dried figs, finely chopped
16 dried apricot halves, cut in half
grated zest of $^1/_2$ orange (optional)
$^1/_4$ cup liquid honey
2 eggs
1 cup buttermilk
60 grams butter, melted

1. Preheat oven to 200°C. Lightly grease 12 muffin tins.
2. Sift together flour, baking powder, baking soda, cinnamon, sugar and salt into a bowl and make a well in the centre.
3. In a bowl combine the figs, apricots, orange zest and honey.
4. In another bowl lightly whisk together eggs, buttermilk and melted butter, and pour over the fig mixture.
5. Fold the fig mixture into the dry ingredients and stir quickly to combine.
6. Spoon mixture into prepared muffin tins and bake for 12–15 minutes or until muffins spring back when lightly pressed.

Makes 12

quite simply, runny honey, raisin and bran muffins

1½ cups baker's bran flakes
1 cup flour
4 teaspoons baking powder
¼ teaspoon salt
½ cup sugar
30 grams butter
2 tablespoons oil
1 cup milk
4 tablespoons liquid honey
½ cup raisins
1 teaspoon baking soda
1 egg, lightly beaten

1. Preheat oven to 200°C. Lightly grease 12 muffin tins.
2. Place bran flakes in a large bowl and sift in the flour, baking powder, salt and sugar.
3. In a small pot gently heat the butter, oil, milk, liquid honey and raisins. Remove from heat, stir in baking soda and allow to cool slightly.
4. Make a well in the centre of the dry ingredients. Pour in the raisin mixture together with the beaten egg. Stir quickly to combine well.
5. Spoon mixture into prepared muffin tins and bake for 12–15 minutes or until muffins spring back when lightly pressed.

Makes 12

oatmeal muffins served with a sauté of orange bananas and a swirl of yoghurt

1 cup rolled oats
1/2 cup sultanas
1/2 cup orange juice or juice of your choice
1 cup flour
2 teaspoons baking powder
1 teaspoon baking soda
1/2 teaspoon salt
1 teaspoon cinnamon
1/2 teaspoon ground cardamom
1/2 cup sugar
60 grams butter, melted
2 eggs
1/2 cup buttermilk

sauté of orange bananas
1 tablespoon butter
2 tablespoons sugar
juice of 1 orange
3 firm bananas, sliced lengthwise and then in half
zest of 1/2 orange
yoghurt to swirl on top

1. Place rolled oats, sultanas and orange juice in a bowl and leave to soak for 30 minutes.

2. Preheat oven to 200°C. Lightly grease 12 muffin tins.

3. Sift together flour, baking powder, baking soda, salt, cinnamon and ground cardamom into a bowl. Stir in sugar and make a well in the centre.

4. In another bowl lightly whisk together the melted butter, eggs and buttermilk. Pour over the soaked oat mixture.

5. Fold oat mixture into dry ingredients and stir quickly to combine.

6. Spoon mixture into prepared muffin tins and bake for 12–15 minutes or until muffins spring back when lightly pressed.

7. To make sauté of orange bananas, gently heat together butter, sugar and orange juice in a small pot. Stir on a low heat until sugar has dissolved.

8. Lay banana slices in pan and sprinkle with the orange zest. Simmer for a couple of minutes.

9. Serve hot, on the side, with a swirl of yoghurt.

Makes 12

shades of green spirulina and banana muffins

2 cups flour
4 teaspoons baking powder
1/2 cup sugar
60 grams butter
4 tablespoons honey
2 eggs
1 1/2 cups fruit yoghurt
1 teaspoon spirulina powder
1 banana, mashed
12 banana slices for topping

1. Preheat oven to 200°C. Lightly grease 12 muffin tins.
2. Sift together flour and baking powder into a bowl, stir in sugar and make a well in the centre.
3. In a small pot melt together the butter and honey.
4. In another bowl lightly whisk together eggs, yoghurt and spirulina.
5. Stir in melted butter and honey and mashed banana.
6. Fold spirulina mixture into dry ingredients and stir quickly to combine.
7. Spoon mixture into prepared muffin tins. Press one banana slice on the top of each muffin and bake for 12–15 minutes or until muffins spring back when lightly pressed.

Makes 12

making a meal
out of it or maybe
a savoury snack

tandoori-topped ginger, pumpkin and mint muffins

2 cups flour
4 teaspoons baking powder
1 teaspoon ground ginger
salt and freshly ground black pepper
60 grams butter, melted
2 eggs
1 cup milk
1 cup cooked pumpkin, lightly salted and mashed
2 tablespoons chopped fresh mint
2 spring onions, chopped
100 grams grated tasty Cheddar cheese
4 tablespoons tandoori paste
25 grams grated tasty Cheddar cheese, to sprinkle on top

L

1. Preheat oven to 210°C. Lightly grease 12 muffin tins.
2. Sift together flour, baking powder, ginger, salt and pepper into a bowl, and make a well in the centre.
3. In another bowl mix together the melted butter, eggs and milk. Stir in the cooked pumpkin, fresh mint, spring onions and cheese.
4. Fold the egg mixture into the dry ingredients and stir quickly to combine.
5. Spoon mixture into prepared muffin tins and top each with one teaspoon of tandoori paste and a sprinkling of cheese.
6. Bake for 12–15 minutes or until muffins spring back when lightly pressed.

Makes 12

provençal tomato, basil and ricotta muffins

1 cup sun-dried tomatoes
2 cups flour
4 teaspoons baking powder
1/4 teaspoon ground nutmeg
pinch of salt
freshly ground black pepper
200 grams ricotta cheese
1/4 cup oil (I use 2 tablespoons oil from the tomatoes
     and 2 tablespoons olive oil)
2 eggs
1 cup milk
2 tablespoons chopped basil leaves

L

1. Preheat oven to 210°C. Lightly grease 12 muffin tins.
2. Place sun-dried tomatoes in a sieve to drain excess oil, then cut into thin strips.
3. Sift flour, baking powder, nutmeg, salt and pepper into a bowl and make a well in the centre.
4. In another bowl lightly whisk together the ricotta cheese, oil, eggs and milk. Stir in sun-dried tomatoes and basil leaves.
5. Fold egg mixture into dry ingredients and stir quickly to combine.
6. Spoon mixture into prepared muffin tins and bake for 12–15 minutes or until muffins spring back when lightly pressed.

Makes 12

smoked salmon with capers and parmesan-crusted top muffins

L

2 cups flour
4 teaspoons baking powder
pinch of salt
freshly ground black pepper
60 grams butter, melted
1 cup milk
2 eggs
50 grams smoked salmon, cut into pieces
225 grams grated mozzarella
4 tablespoons capers
2 tablespoons grated Parmesan cheese

1. Preheat oven to 210°C. Lightly grease 12 muffin tins.
2. Sift together flour, baking powder, salt and pepper into a bowl and make a well in the centre.
3. In another bowl lightly whisk together the melted butter, milk and eggs. Stir in the smoked salmon, mozzarella and capers.
4. Fold the egg mixture into the dry ingredients and stir quickly to combine.
5. Spoon mixture evenly into prepared muffin tins and sprinkle Parmesan cheese on top of each muffin.
6. Bake for 12–15 minutes or until muffins spring back when lightly pressed.

Makes 12

caramelised onion and chorizo muffins with parsley butter

caramelised onion

2 medium red onions, sliced
2 teaspoons olive oil
4 tablespoons balsamic vinegar
2 tablespoons liquid honey
1 tablespoon icing sugar

muffin batter

3 cups flour
2 tablespoons baking powder
2 teaspoons cumin
salt and freshly ground black pepper
1 egg
1¼ cups milk
150 grams grated tasty Cheddar cheese
100 grams grated mozzarella cheese
1 chorizo sausage, chopped

parsley butter – refer page 154

1. Preheat oven to 210°C. Lightly grease 12 muffin tins.
2. To caramelise onions, heat oil in a non-stick pan and sauté onions until soft. Add balsamic vinegar, honey and icing sugar and cook until liquid is absorbed. Cool.
3. Sift together flour, baking powder, cumin, salt and pepper into a bowl and make a well in the centre.
4. In another bowl lightly whisk together the egg and milk. Stir in the Cheddar and mozzarella cheeses and chorizo sausage.

5. Reserve 4 tablespoons of caramelised onion for the topping and fold the remaining onion into the egg mixture.
6. Fold the egg mixture into the dry ingredients and stir quickly to combine.
7. Spoon mixture into prepared muffin tins. Top each muffin with a teaspoon of caramelised onion and bake for 12–15 minutes or until muffins spring back when lightly pressed.

Makes 12

ham, cheese and pineapple muffins

2 cups flour
4 teaspoons baking powder
$^1/_2$ teaspoon salt
2 eggs
1 cup milk
100 grams ham, chopped
200 grams grated tasty Cheddar cheese
1 cup pineapple pieces, well-drained and roughly chopped

L

1. Preheat oven to 210°C. Lightly grease 12 muffin tins.
2. Sift together flour, baking powder and salt into a bowl and make a well in the centre.
3. In another bowl lightly whisk together the eggs and milk. Stir in the ham, cheese and pineapple.
4. Fold the egg mixture into dry ingredients and stir quickly to combine.
5. Spoon mixture into prepared muffin tins and bake for 12–15 minutes or until muffins spring back when lightly pressed.

Makes 12

simple sweetcorn muffins

1 cup flour
2 teaspoons baking powder
1/4 teaspoon cayenne pepper
1/2 teaspoon salt
2 teaspoons sugar
40 grams butter, melted
2 eggs
1/2 cup milk
1 x 410g can sweetcorn, drained
1/2 red pepper, cut into small pieces
4 spring onions, finely chopped
handful of chopped parsley

1. Preheat oven to 210°C. Lightly grease 8 muffin tins.
2. Sift flour, baking powder, cayenne pepper, salt and sugar into a bowl, and make a well in the centre.
3. In a bowl lightly whisk together the melted butter, eggs and milk. Stir in the sweetcorn, red pepper, spring onions and parsley.
4. Fold egg mixture into dry ingredients and stir quickly to combine.
5. Spoon mixture into prepared muffin tins and bake for 12–15 minutes or until muffins spring back when lightly pressed.

Makes 8

These muffins are great on the side. I serve them with roasted chicken, vegetables and gravy – delicious! Could also be served for breakfast with crispy strips of bacon.

broccoli and bacon muffins

1 medium head broccoli, cut into small florets
4 rashers bacon, finely chopped
1 medium onion, finely chopped
2 cups flour
4 teaspoons baking powder
$1/2$ teaspoon salt
freshly ground black pepper
150 grams grated tasty Cheddar cheese
2 eggs
1 cup milk

L

1. Preheat oven to 210°C. Lightly grease 12 muffin tins.
2. Place broccoli florets in a pot, cover with boiling water and boil for 2 minutes. Refresh under cold water and pat dry on a paper towel.
3. Heat a non-stick pan and sauté bacon and onion until tender. Set aside to cool.
4. Sift together flour, baking powder, salt and pepper into a bowl and make a well in the centre.
5. In another bowl lightly whisk together eggs and milk.
6. Stir in broccoli, bacon, onion and cheese.
7. Fold broccoli mixture into dry ingredients and stir quickly to combine.
8. Spoon mixture into prepared muffin tins and bake for 12–15 minutes or until muffins spring back when lightly pressed.

Makes 12

avocado, cheese and sunflower seed muffins

1 cup flour
2 teaspoons baking powder
1/4 teaspoon salt
freshly ground black pepper
1 egg
1/2 cup milk
1/2 avocado, cut into cubes
125 grams grated tasty Cheddar cheese
handful of parsley, roughly chopped
1/2 red pepper, chopped
2 tablespoons sunflower seeds

L

1. Preheat oven to 210°C. Lightly grease 6 muffin tins.
2. Sift together flour, baking powder, salt and pepper into a bowl and make a well in the centre.
3. In another bowl lightly whisk together the egg and milk. Stir in avocado, cheese, parsley and red pepper.
4. Fold egg mixture into dry ingredients and stir quickly to combine.
5. Spoon mixture into prepared muffin tins and fill empty muffin cups with water to prevent buckling.
6. Sprinkle sunflower seeds on top of each muffin.
7. Bake for 12–15 minutes or until muffins spring back when lightly pressed.

Makes 6

green onion, sour cream and corn muffins

1 cup flour
1 cup cornmeal
3 teaspoons baking powder
$1/2$ teaspoon baking soda
$1/2$ teaspoon salt
freshly ground black pepper
4 tablespoons sour cream
2 eggs
$3/4$ cup milk
2 teaspoons sweet chilli sauce
6 spring onions, trimmed and finely chopped
6 rashers bacon, grilled and chopped
2 cups sweetcorn, drained

L

1. Preheat oven to 210°C. Lightly grease 12 muffin tins.
2. Sift the flour, cornmeal, baking powder, baking soda, salt and pepper into a bowl and make a well in the centre.
3. In another bowl lightly whisk together the sour cream, eggs, milk and sweet chilli sauce. Stir in the spring onions, bacon and sweetcorn.
4. Fold egg mixture into dry ingredients and stir quickly to combine.
5. Spoon mixture into prepared muffin tins and bake for 12–15 minutes or until muffins spring back when lightly pressed.

Makes 12

roasted pear, goats' cheese and prosciutto
muffins

2 pears, peeled, cored and cut into quarters
2 tablespoons balsamic vinegar
2 teaspoons soft brown sugar
2 cups flour
4 teaspoons baking powder
pinch of salt
$1/4$ cup olive oil
2 eggs
1 cup milk
150 grams goats' feta or blue vein cheese
4 slices prosciutto
1 unpeeled pear for topping, quartered, cored and cut into thin slices

1. Preheat oven to 210°C. Lightly grease 12 muffin tins.
2. Place peeled pears in an ovenproof dish, brush with balsamic vinegar and sprinkle with the sugar. Roast in the oven for 10–15 minutes. Remove and allow to cool, then cut into chunks.
3. Sift together the flour, baking powder and salt into a bowl and make a well in the centre.
4. In another bowl lightly whisk together the oil, eggs and milk. Stir in the chopped pears, feta cheese and prosciutto.
5. Fold egg mixture into dry ingredients and stir quickly to combine.
6. Spoon mixture into prepared muffin tins. Fan unpeeled pear slices on top of each muffin. Bake for 12–15 minutes or until muffins spring back when lightly pressed.

Makes 12

south of the border guacamole muffins

1½ cups flour
3 teaspoons baking powder
½ teaspoon salt
freshly ground black pepper
2 ripe avocados
juice of 1 lemon
1 small red onion, finely chopped
¼ cup sun-dried tomatoes, chopped
6 dashes of Tabasco sauce or 1 teaspoon sweet chilli sauce
1 egg
¼ cup olive oil
¾ cup milk

S

1. Preheat oven to 210°C. Lightly grease 12 muffin tins.
2. Sift flour, baking powder, salt and pepper into a bowl and make a well in the centre.
3. Cut avocados in half, remove stone, spoon flesh out of shell and chop into small chunks. Place avocado in a bowl and cover with lemon juice to prevent browning. Mix in the onion, sun-dried tomatoes and Tabasco sauce.
4. In another bowl whisk together the egg, oil and milk, and pour into the avocado mixture.
5. Pour the egg mixture into dry ingredients and stir quickly to combine.
6. Spoon mixture evenly into prepared muffin tins and bake for 12–15 minutes or until muffins spring back when lightly pressed.

Makes 12

Making a meal of it:
Split the muffin and fill with crispy green lettuce and layers of shaved ham.

mamma mia muffins

2 cups flour
4 teaspoons baking powder
1/4 teaspoon salt
freshly ground black pepper
1/4 cup olive oil
1 egg
1 cup milk
1/2 cup sun-dried tomatoes, chopped
8 black olives, stoned and sliced
150 grams feta cheese, chopped into small pieces
1/4 cup fresh basil, roughly chopped

topping
25 grams grated Parmesan cheese
6 olives, stoned and cut in half for top of each muffin

1. Preheat oven to 210°C. Lightly grease 12 muffin tins.
2. Sift together flour, baking powder, salt and pepper into a bowl and make a well in the centre.
3. In another bowl lightly whisk together the oil, egg and milk. Stir in the sun-dried tomatoes, olives, feta cheese and basil.
4. Fold egg mixture into the dry ingredients and stir quickly to combine.
5. Spoon mixture into prepared muffin tins, sprinkle a little Parmesan cheese on top of each muffin and press half an olive into the mixture.
6. Bake for 12–15 minutes or until muffins spring back when lightly pressed.

Makes 12

spinach, lemon and pine nut muffins

2 cups flour
4 teaspoons baking powder
freshly ground black pepper
1 teaspoon salt
3 tightly packed cups fresh spinach leaves, washed, dried and thinly sliced
2 eggs
$^3/_4$ cup milk
200 grams grated tasty Cheddar cheese
2 tablespoons lemon juice
zest of $^1/_2$ lemon
2 tablespoons basil pesto
4 tablespoons pine nuts

1. Preheat oven to 210°C. Lightly grease 12 muffin tins.
2. Sift flour, baking powder and pepper into a bowl and make a well in the centre.
3. Sprinkle salt over sliced spinach.
4. In another bowl lightly whisk together the eggs and milk. Stir in the spinach, Cheddar cheese, lemon juice, lemon zest and basil pesto.
5. Fold the egg mixture into the dry ingredients and stir quickly to combine.
6. Spoon mixture evenly into prepared muffin tins, top each muffin with one teaspoon of pine nuts and bake for 12–15 minutes or until muffins spring back when lightly pressed.

Makes 12

forty roasted cloves of garlic muffins

40 large cloves of garlic, unpeeled
1 teaspoon oil
2 cups flour
4 teaspoons baking powder
1 teaspoon salt
freshly ground black pepper
1 cup milk
2 eggs
300 grams grated tasty Cheddar cheese
$1/2$ cup chopped parsley

L

1. Preheat oven to 210°C. Lightly grease 12 muffin tins.
2. Place garlic cloves in an ovenproof dish, brush with oil and roast for 10 minutes. Allow to slightly cool, remove skin and chop into small pieces.
3. Sift together flour, baking powder, salt and pepper into a bowl and make a well in the centre.
4. In another bowl lightly whisk together the milk and eggs. Stir in garlic cloves, grated cheese and parsley.
5. Fold egg mixture into dry ingredients and stir quickly to combine.
6. Spoon mixture evenly into prepared muffin tins and bake for 12–15 minutes or until muffins spring back when lightly pressed.

Makes 12

pastrami pesto muffins

L

2 cups flour
4 teaspoons baking powder
pinch of salt and freshly ground black pepper
2 eggs
1 cup milk
175 grams grated tasty Cheddar cheese
2 tablespoons basil pesto
100 grams pastrami, chopped
1 tablespoon chopped fresh basil

1. Preheat oven to 210°C. Lightly grease 12 muffin tins.
2. Sift together flour, baking powder, salt and pepper into a bowl and make a well in the centre.
3. In another bowl lightly whisk together the eggs and milk. Stir in the grated cheese, pesto, pastrami and fresh basil.
4. Fold the egg mixture into the dry ingredients and stir quickly to combine.
5. Spoon mixture evenly into prepared muffin tins and bake for 12–15 minutes or until muffins spring back when lightly pressed.

Makes 12

If you want to make your own basil pesto, you will find my recipe on page 155. If you prefer, simply buy a commercial variety from the supermarket.

celery and cheese muffins

1 cup flour
2 teaspoons baking powder
$^1/_4$ teaspoon salt
freshly ground black pepper
1 egg
$^1/_2$ cup milk
1 teaspoon seed mustard
2 sticks celery, chopped
2 spring onions, chopped
150 grams grated tasty Cheddar cheese
handful of chopped parsley
1 teaspoon dried oregano

L

1. Preheat oven to 210°C. Lightly grease 6 muffin tins.
2. Sift together flour, baking powder, salt and pepper into a bowl and make a well in the centre.
3. In another bowl whisk together the egg, milk and seed mustard. Stir in the celery, spring onions, cheese, parsley and oregano.
4. Fold cheese mixture into dry ingredients and stir quickly to combine.
5. Spoon mixture into prepared muffin tins and bake for 12–15 minutes or until muffins spring back when lightly pressed.

Makes 6

Just a thought:
When it is just the two of us at home, I find it handy to be able to whip up these six muffins. If you need more, then the recipe will easily double to make 12 muffins.

hash brown, egg and bacon wrap muffins

6 rashers streaky bacon
1 cup flour
2 teaspoons baking powder
$1/2$ teaspoon salt
$1/2$ cup grated potato, squeezed to remove excess liquid
2 tablespoons olive oil (or use oil from sun-dried tomatoes)
$1/2$ cup milk
2 tablespoons sun-dried tomatoes, finely chopped
handful of chopped parsley
freshly ground black pepper
6 small eggs
salt and freshly ground black pepper to season eggs

L

1. Preheat oven to 210°C. Lightly grease 6 muffin tins.
2. Place one rasher of bacon across each muffin tin. (The rasher will look too long but the ends will be wrapped over the muffin before baking.)
3. Sift together flour and baking powder into a bowl and make a well in the centre. Sprinkle the half teaspoon of salt over the grated potato.
4. In another bowl lightly whisk together the oil and milk. Stir in the grated potato, sun-dried tomatoes, parsley and pepper.
5. Fold potato mixture into dry ingredients and stir quickly to combine. (The mixture looks strange, but don't panic.)
6. Half fill the bacon-lined tins with the muffin mixture and break one egg on top of each. Lightly pepper and salt, and top with remaining mixture.
7. Wrap bacon strips over the top of the muffins and bake for 15–20 minutes or until risen and bacon is crispy.

Makes 6

Make a meal out of it:
Great for school lunches, taking to work or for picnics.

smoked salmon and mature cheese muffins

2 cups flour
4 teaspoons baking powder
pinch of salt and freshly ground black pepper
2 eggs
1 cup milk
200 grams grated mature Cheddar cheese
100 grams smoked salmon, sliced
1/2 cup chopped parsley

1. Preheat oven to 210°C. Lightly grease 12 muffin tins.
2. Sift together flour, baking powder, salt and pepper into a bowl and make a well in the centre.
3. In another bowl lightly whisk together the eggs and milk.
4. Stir in the grated cheese, smoked salmon and parsley.
5. Fold egg mixture into dry ingredients and stir quickly to combine.
6. Spoon mixture evenly into prepared muffin tins and bake for 12–15 minutes or until muffins spring back when lightly pressed.
7. Serve with lime chilli butter (refer page 154).

Makes 12

crunchy peanut satay muffins

2 cups flour
4 teaspoons baking powder
1 tablespoon medium curry powder
$1/2$ teaspoon salt
freshly ground black pepper
8 teaspoons crunchy peanut butter
$1/2$ cup oil
2 teaspoons sweet chilli sauce
2 eggs
$3/4$ cup coconut milk
$1/2$ red onion, finely chopped
$1/2$ cup roasted red pepper, cut into chunks
$1/2$ cup aduki sprouts
$1/4$ cup chopped peanuts for topping

S

1. Preheat oven to 210°C. Lightly grease 12 muffin tins.
2. Sift together flour, baking powder, curry powder, salt and pepper into a bowl and make a well in the centre.
3. In a pot gently heat peanut butter, oil and sweet chilli sauce.
4. In another bowl lightly whisk together eggs and coconut milk. Add melted peanut butter mixture and stir in red onion, red pepper and aduki sprouts.
5. Fold egg mixture into dry ingredients and stir quickly to combine.
6. Spoon mixture evenly into prepared muffin tins and sprinkle one teaspoon of chopped peanuts on top of each muffin.
7. Bake for 12–15 minutes or until muffins spring back when lightly pressed.

Makes 12

salami and olive pizza muffins

2 cups flour
4 teaspoons baking powder
$^1/_2$ teaspoon baking soda
1 egg
$^1/_4$ cup olive oil
$^1/_2$ cup milk
$^1/_2$ cup natural yoghurt
100 grams salami, cut into small pieces
100 grams mozzarella, grated
$^1/_2$ cup chargrilled red peppers in oil, drained and chopped
10 black olives, stoned and thinly sliced

L

topping
4 tablespoons tomato paste
25 grams grated tasty Cheddar cheese

1. Preheat oven to 210°C. Lightly grease 12 muffin tins.
2. Sift together flour, baking powder and baking soda into a bowl and make a well in the centre.
3. In another bowl lightly whisk together the egg, olive oil, milk and yoghurt. Stir in the salami, mozzarella, peppers and olives.
4. Fold egg mixture into dry ingredients and stir quickly to combine.
5. Spoon mixture into prepared muffin tins. Spread each muffin with one teaspoon of tomato paste and sprinkle with cheese.
6. Bake for 12–15 minutes or until muffins spring back when lightly pressed and cheese is golden brown.

Makes 12

a ploughman's, a beer and it's lunch muffins

L

2 cups flour
4 teaspoons baking powder
1/2 teaspoon salt
1 tablespoon seed mustard
2 eggs
1 cup beer
200 grams grated mature Cheddar cheese
8 pickled onions, thinly sliced
1 tablespoon chopped chives

1. Preheat oven to 210°C. Lightly grease 12 muffin tins.
2. Sift together flour, baking powder and salt into a bowl and make a well in the centre.
3. In another bowl lightly whisk together the mustard, eggs and beer.
4. Sir in the cheese, pickled onions and chives.
5. Fold egg mixture into dry ingredients and stir quickly to combine.
6. Spoon mixture into prepared muffin tins and bake for 12–15 minutes or until muffins spring back when lightly pressed.

Makes 12

polka dots of minted peas and ham muffins

2 cups flour
4 teaspoons baking powder
freshly ground black pepper
$^{1}/_{2}$ teaspoon salt
$1^{1}/_{2}$ cups frozen peas, slightly thawed
$^{1}/_{4}$ cup chopped fresh mint
$^{1}/_{4}$ cup olive oil
2 eggs
1 cup milk
200 grams chopped ham

L

1. Preheat the oven to 210°C. Lightly grease 12 muffin tins.
2. Sift together flour, baking powder and black pepper into a bowl and make a well in the centre.
3. Sprinkle salt over peas and add mint.
4. In another bowl lightly whisk together the oil, eggs and milk. Stir in the salted peas, mint and ham.
5. Fold egg mixture into dry ingredients and stir quickly to combine.
6. Spoon mixture into prepared muffin tins and bake for 12–15 minutes or until muffins spring back when lightly pressed.

Makes 12

walnuts and blue cheese muffins served with fresh pear slices

2 cups flour
4 teaspoons baking powder
$1/4$ teaspoon salt
freshly ground black pepper
60 grams butter, melted
2 eggs
1 cup milk
$1/2$ cup chopped walnuts
150 grams blue cheese, crumbled
fresh pears, sliced, to serve on side

1. Preheat oven to 210°C. Lightly grease 12 muffin tins.
2. Sift together flour, baking powder, salt and pepper into a bowl and make a well in the centre.
3. In another bowl lightly whisk together the melted butter, eggs and milk. Stir in walnuts and crumbled blue cheese.
4. Fold cheese mixture into dry ingredients and stir quickly to combine.
5. Spoon mixture into prepared muffin tins and bake for 12–15 minutes or until muffins spring back when lightly pressed.
6. Serve with fresh pear slices on the side.

Makes 12

bangers and mash muffins

2 cups flour
4 teaspoons baking powder
1/4 teaspoon salt
1/4 cup HP sauce or tomato chutney
60 grams butter, melted
1 cup milk
2 eggs
1 cup lightly salted mashed potato
3 sausages, boiled, skinned and cut into small chunks
4 spring onions, chopped
extra HP sauce for glaze

L

1. Preheat the oven to 210°C. Lightly grease 12 muffin tins.
2. Sift together flour, baking powder and salt into a bowl and make a well in the centre.
3. In another bowl lightly whisk together the HP sauce, melted butter, milk and eggs. Stir in the mashed potato, sausages and spring onions.
4. Fold egg mixture into dry ingredients and stir quickly to combine.
5. Spoon mixture evenly into prepared muffin tins and lightly brush top of each muffin with HP sauce to glaze.
6. Bake for 12–15 minutes or until muffins spring back when lightly pressed.

Makes 12

zucchini and cheese muffins filled with tomato salsa

1 cup flour
2 teaspoons baking powder
freshly ground black pepper
$^1/_2$ teaspoon salt
4 zucchini, grated
2 eggs
$^1/_2$ cup milk
150 grams grated tasty Cheddar cheese

tomato salsa – refer page 151

1. Preheat oven to 210°C. Lightly grease 10 muffin tins.
2. Sift together flour, baking powder and pepper into a bowl and make a well in the centre.
3. Sprinkle salt over the grated zucchini.
4. In another bowl lightly whisk together the eggs and milk. Stir in the grated zucchini and cheese.
5. Fold the egg mixture into dry ingredients and stir quickly to combine.
6. Spoon the mixture into prepared muffin tins and bake for 12–15 minutes or until muffins spring back when lightly pressed.
7. Serve with tomato salsa.

Makes 10

sometimes I just want a cheese muffin

1¼ cups flour
1 dessertspoon baking powder
pinch of salt
¼ teaspoon cayenne pepper
1 egg
¾ cup milk
100 grams grated tasty Cheddar cheese

L

1. Preheat oven to 210°C. Lightly grease 6 muffin tins.
2. Sift together flour, baking powder, salt and cayenne pepper into a bowl and make a well in the centre.
3. In another bowl lightly whisk together the egg and milk. Stir in the grated cheese.
4. Fold egg mixture into dry ingredients and stir quickly to combine.
5. Spoon mixture into prepared muffin tins.
6. Bake for 12–15 minutes or until muffins spring back when lightly pressed.

Makes 6

This recipe is a good basic which can, if you wish, be upgraded by simply adding a combination of ingredients such as chopped spring onions, red or green peppers, ham or cooked bacon – but some days you can't beat leaving it plain.

kumara and bacon muffins

2 cups flour
4 teaspoons baking powder
¹/₄ teaspoon salt
freshly ground black pepper
2 eggs
1 cup milk
1 cup kumara, boiled in lightly salted water, drained and mashed
200 grams grated tasty Cheddar cheese
1 medium onion, finely chopped
2 rashers bacon, grilled and chopped
handful of chopped parsley

L

1. Preheat oven to 210°C. Lightly grease 12 muffin tins.
2. Sift together flour, baking powder, salt and pepper into a bowl and make a well in the centre.
3. In another bowl lightly whisk together the eggs and milk. Stir in the kumara, cheese, onion, bacon and parsley.
4. Fold the egg mixture into dry ingredients and stir quickly to combine.
5. Spoon mixture evenly into prepared muffin tins and bake for 12–15 minutes or until muffins spring back when lightly pressed.

Makes 12

cauliflower cheese crumble muffins

2 cups cauliflower florets, chopped small

L

2 cups flour
4 teaspoons baking powder
1 teaspoon chicken stock powder
1/2 teaspoon salt
freshly ground black pepper
2 eggs
1 cup milk
2 teaspoons seed mustard
250 grams grated tasty Cheddar cheese
1 medium onion, very finely chopped
1/4 cup dried breadcrumbs for topping

1. Preheat oven to 210°C. Lightly grease 12 muffin tins.
2. Place cauliflower in a pot and cover with boiling water. Lightly salt, then boil for 5 minutes. Remove from heat, drain and refresh under cold water. Pat dry on a paper towel and allow to cool.
3. Sift together flour, baking powder, chicken stock powder, salt and pepper into a bowl and make a well in the centre.
4. In another bowl lightly whisk together the eggs, milk and seed mustard.
5. Stir in the cauliflower, grated cheese and onion.
6. Fold cauliflower mixture into dry ingredients and stir quickly to combine.
7. Spoon mixture into prepared muffin tins. Sprinkle each muffin with dried breadcrumbs and bake for 12–15 minutes or until muffins spring back when lightly pressed.

Makes 12

a weekend brunch of grilled bacon and maple banana muffins

2 cups flour
4 teaspoons baking powder
2 bananas, peeled and sliced
2 tablespoons maple syrup
60 grams butter, melted
2 eggs
1 cup milk
6 rashers bacon, grilled and chopped

L

1. Preheat oven to 210°C. Lightly grease 12 muffin tins.
2. Sift together flour and baking powder into a bowl and make a well in the centre.
3. Place sliced bananas in a small bowl and coat with maple syrup.
4. In another bowl lightly whisk together melted butter, eggs and milk. Stir in bacon and banana.
5. Fold the egg mixture into the dry ingredients and stir quickly to combine.
6. Spoon mixture into prepared muffin tins and bake for 12–15 minutes or until muffins spring back when lightly pressed.

Makes 12

sautéed leek, apple and caraway seed muffins

2 teaspoons butter
2 Granny Smith apples, peeled, cored and cubed
1 leek, washed, trimmed and diced
1 teaspoon caraway seeds
1³/₄ cups flour
2 teaspoons baking powder
¹/₂ teaspoon baking soda
pinch of salt and freshly ground black pepper
³/₄ cup milk
2 teaspoons lemon juice or vinegar
60 grams butter, melted
1 egg

1. Preheat oven to 210°C. Lightly grease 12 muffin tins.
2. Place 2 teaspoons of butter in a non-stick pan, add apples, leek and caraway seeds and sauté until tender. Allow to cool.
3. Sift together flour, baking powder, baking soda, salt and pepper into a bowl and make a well in the centre.
4. Pour milk and lemon juice into another bowl and leave to sour for about 5 minutes. Whisk in the melted butter and egg. Stir in the sautéed apples, leek and caraway seeds.
5. Fold the egg mixture into the dry ingredients and stir quickly to combine.
6. Spoon mixture into prepared muffin tins and bake for 12–15 minutes or until muffins spring back when lightly pressed.

Makes 12

feta and bacon muffins with maple cream cheese spread

2 cups flour
4 teaspoons baking powder
pinch of salt and freshly ground black pepper
2 eggs
1 cup milk
2 tablespoons seed mustard
100 grams feta cheese, crumbled
100 grams grated tasty Cheddar cheese
2 rashers bacon, chopped
1 medium onion, finely chopped
handful of chopped parsley

L

maple cream cheese spread
1/4 cup cream cheese
4 teaspoons maple syrup
freshly ground black pepper

1. Preheat oven to 210°C. Lightly grease 12 muffin tins.
2. Sift together flour, baking powder, salt and pepper into a bowl and make a well in the centre.
3. In another bowl lightly whisk together the eggs, milk and seed mustard. Stir in the feta cheese, Cheddar cheese, bacon, onion and parsley.
4. Fold egg mixture into dry ingredients and stir quickly to combine.
5. Spoon the mixture evenly into prepared muffin tins and bake for 12–15 minutes or until muffins spring back when lightly pressed.
6. To make the maple cream cheese spread, mix all the ingredients together and serve on the side with the muffins.

Makes 12

smoked mussels and crispy bacon muffins

2 cups flour
4 teaspoons baking powder
1/4 teaspoon salt
freshly ground black pepper
1/4 cup olive oil
2 eggs
1 cup milk
200 grams smoked mussels, chopped
4 rashers bacon, grilled and chopped
handful of chopped parsley

1. Preheat oven to 210°C. Lightly grease 12 muffin tins.
2. Sift together flour, baking powder, salt and pepper into a bowl and make a well in the centre.
3. In another bowl lightly whisk together the olive oil, eggs and milk. Stir in smoked mussels, three-quarters of the bacon (reserving some for the top) and parsley.
4. Fold egg mixture into dry ingredients and stir quickly to combine.
5. Spoon mixture into prepared muffin tins, top with reserved chopped bacon and bake for 12–15 minutes or until muffins spring back when lightly pressed.

Make a meal out of it:
Serve with a crisp green side salad and chunks of tomatoes, cucumber and chopped fresh basil.

chilli zucchini muffins with a dusting of parmesan cheese

1½ cups flour
½ cup cornmeal
3 teaspoons baking powder
½ teaspoon baking soda
¼ teaspoon salt
2 cups grated zucchini
1 tablespoon sweet chilli sauce
¼ cup olive oil
1 cup buttermilk
2 eggs
2 tablespoons freshly grated Parmesan cheese

$$\boxed{S}$$

1. Preheat oven to 210°C. Lightly grease 12 muffin tins.
2. Sift together flour, cornmeal, baking powder and baking soda into a bowl and make a well in the centre. Sprinkle salt over grated zucchini.
3. In another bowl lightly whisk together the sweet chilli sauce, olive oil, buttermilk and eggs. Stir in grated zucchini.
4. Fold egg mixture into dry ingredients and stir quickly to combine.
5. Spoon mixture into prepared muffin tins. Sprinkle each muffin with a dusting of Parmesan cheese.
6. Bake for 12–15 minutes or until muffins spring back when lightly pressed.

Makes 12

This muffin is ideal for those of you who enjoy a savoury snack, or it could be served on the side with soup.

home alone fresh herbs and cheese muffins

1 egg
2 tablespoons milk
1 teaspoon seed mustard
25 grams grated tasty Cheddar cheese
1 small onion, finely chopped
2 teaspoons flour
$\frac{1}{2}$ teaspoon baking powder
2 tablespoons dried breadcrumbs
handful of chopped fresh herbs, (e.g. parsley or oregano)
pinch of salt
freshly ground black pepper

L

1. Preheat oven to 210°C. Lightly grease 3 muffin tins.
2. In a bowl lightly whisk together the egg, milk and seed mustard.
3. Stir in grated cheese, onion, sifted flour and baking powder,
   breadcrumbs, fresh herbs, salt and pepper.
4. Spoon mixture into prepared muffin tins.
5. Bake for 12–15 minutes or until muffins spring back when lightly
   pressed.

Makes 3

Just a thought:
This recipe could easily be doubled.

corned beef and chow chow pickle muffins

2 cups flour
4 teaspoons baking powder
pinch of salt and freshly ground black pepper
$1/4$ cup olive oil
2 eggs
$3/4$ cup milk
200 grams corned beef, chopped into small pieces
$1/2$ cup chow chow pickle

L

1. Preheat oven to 210°C. Lightly grease 12 muffin tins.
2. Sift together flour, baking powder, salt and pepper into a bowl and make a well in the centre.
3. In another bowl lightly whisk together the oil, eggs and milk. Stir in corned beef and pickle.
4. Fold egg mixture into dry ingredients and stir quickly to combine.
5. Spoon mixture into prepared muffin tins and bake for 12–15 minutes or until muffins spring back when lightly pressed.

Makes 12

cornmeal with blue cheese and bacon muffins

1 cup cornmeal
1 cup flour
2 teaspoons baking powder
1 teaspoon baking soda
$1/4$ teaspoon salt
freshly ground black pepper
$1/4$ cup olive oil
2 eggs
1 cup buttermilk
handful of chopped parsley
4 rashers bacon, grilled and chopped
150 grams blue cheese, crumbled

L

1. Preheat oven to 210°C. Lightly grease 12 muffin tins.
2. Sift together cornmeal, flour, baking powder, baking soda, salt and pepper into a bowl.
3. In another bowl lightly whisk together the olive oil, eggs and buttermilk. Stir in parsley, bacon and crumbled blue cheese.
4. Fold bacon mixture into dry ingredients and stir quickly to combine.
5. Spoon mixture into prepared muffin tins and bake for 12–15 minutes or until muffins spring back when lightly pressed.

Makes 12

roasted asparagus and prosciutto muffins

12 spears fresh asparagus
1 teaspoon olive oil
$^1/_2$ teaspoon salt
2 cups flour
4 teaspoons baking powder
$^1/_4$ teaspoon salt
freshly ground black pepper
2 eggs
$^1/_4$ cup olive oil
1 cup milk
100 grams sliced prosciutto
100 grams grated Gruyère cheese

L

1. Preheat oven to 210°C. Lightly grease 12 muffin tins.
2. Snap the woody ends off the bottoms of the asparagus. Remove the top 3cm and reserve uncooked for topping. Brush stalks with oil, sprinkle with salt and place in oven for 10 minutes. Remove and allow to cool. Chop the roasted stalks into small chunks.
3. Sift together flour, baking powder, salt and pepper into a bowl and make a well in the centre.
4. In another bowl lightly whisk together the eggs, oil and milk. Stir in the asparagus pieces, prosciutto and Gruyère cheese.
5. Fold the egg mixture into dry ingredients and stir quickly to combine.
6. Spoon mixture into prepared muffin tins, press the uncooked reserved asparagus spear into the top of each muffin and bake for 12–15 minutes or until muffins spring back when lightly pressed.

Makes 12

why not a yorkshire muffin?

³/₄ cup flour
pinch of salt and freshly ground black pepper
1 egg
¹/₂ cup milk
¹/₄ cup water
1 tablespoon very finely chopped parsley
4 teaspoons oil

S

1. Preheat oven to 220°C. Lightly grease 8 muffin tins.
2. Sift together flour, salt and pepper into a bowl and make a well in the centre.
3. Drop in egg and begin to whisk the egg into the flour.
4. Mix together the milk, water and parsley, and gradually whisk into the mixture. Cover and leave the mixture to stand for about 10 minutes.
5. Spoon half a teaspoon of oil into each of the 8 muffin tins and place in the oven to preheat for about 5 minutes. Turn stove top element onto a medium heat, remove muffin tin from oven and place directly on to element.
6. Spoon Yorkshire muffin mixture evenly into prepared muffin tins and place in the oven on a high shelf (about 2 rungs down from the top). Turn off stove element.
7. Bake for 20–23 minutes or until golden and crisp. Serve on the side of roast beef.

Makes 8

sweet as

orange and lemon poppy seed muffins with a zesty glaze

2 cups flour
3 teaspoons baking powder
$1/2$ cup poppy seeds
juice of 1 orange
milk to bring orange juice to 1 cup
zest of 1 orange and 1 lemon (half for muffin and half for topping)
2 eggs
60 grams butter, melted

zesty glaze
juice of 1 lemon
$1/4$ cup sugar
remaining orange and lemon zest

1. Preheat oven to 200°C. Lightly grease 12 muffin tins.
2. Sift together flour and baking powder into a bowl, stir in poppy seeds and make a well in the centre.
3. Pour squeezed orange juice into a measuring jug and make up to 1 cup with milk. Stir in half the orange and lemon zest.
4. In another bowl lightly whisk eggs and melted butter, and pour into the juice mixture. Fold egg mixture into dry ingredients and stir quickly to combine.
5. Spoon mixture into prepared muffin tins and bake for 12–15 minutes or until muffins spring back when lightly pressed.
6. To make the zesty glaze, stir lemon juice, sugar and remaining zest together in a small pot. Gently heat until sugar dissolves, cool slightly and pour over muffins.

Makes 12

pumpkin, fig and pine nut muffins with a ginger streusel

2 cups pumpkin, cooked and mashed
2 cups flour
4 teaspoons baking powder
1 teaspoon cinnamon
$1/2$ teaspoon ground nutmeg
$1/4$ teaspoon ground cloves
pinch of salt
$1/2$ cup soft brown sugar
60 grams butter, melted
2 eggs
1 cup milk
8 dried figs, stems removed, cut into small chunks
4 tablespoons pine nuts

ginger streusel
$1/2$ cup flour
1 teaspoon ground ginger
2 tablespoons butter, softened
$1/4$ cup soft brown sugar
$1/2$ cup crystallised ginger, chopped

1. Preheat oven to 200°C. Lightly grease 12 muffin tins.
2. Place pumpkin in a bowl and stir in sifted flour, baking powder, cinnamon, nutmeg, cloves and salt. Stir in sugar and make a well in the centre.
3. In another bowl lightly whisk together the melted butter, eggs and milk. Stir in figs and pine nuts.
4. Fold fig mixture into dry ingredients and stir quickly to combine.
5. Spoon mixture into prepared muffin tins.

6. To prepare the ginger streusel, sift together flour and ground ginger into a bowl and rub in butter with fingertips. Stir in the sugar and crystallised ginger.
7. Sprinkle streusel evenly over the 12 muffins and bake for 12–15 minutes or until muffins spring back when lightly pressed.

Makes 12

peaches and cream cheese muffins

2 cups flour
4 teaspoons baking powder
$^1/_4$ cup sugar
60 grams butter, melted
2 eggs
$^3/_4$ cup milk
1 cup canned peaches, drained (reserve syrup) and chopped
$^1/_2$ cup peach syrup
12 teaspoons cream cheese

1. Preheat oven to 200°C. Lightly grease 12 muffin tins.
2. Sift together flour and baking powder into a bowl, stir in sugar and make a well in the centre.
3. In another bowl lightly whisk together the melted butter, eggs and milk. Stir in the peaches and peach syrup.
4. Fold peach mixture into dry ingredients and stir quickly to combine.
5. Spoon one tablespoon of mixture into prepared muffin tins, top with one teaspoon of cream cheese and cover with remaining muffin mixture.
6. Bake for 12–15 minutes or until muffins spring back when lightly pressed.

Makes 12

walnut banana muffins

2 cups flour
2 teaspoons baking powder
1 teaspoon baking soda
1 teaspoon cinnamon
$^1/_2$ cup soft brown sugar
60 grams butter, melted
1 teaspoon vanilla essence
1 egg
1 cup buttermilk
2 bananas, peeled and mashed
$^1/_2$ cup chopped walnuts
1 banana, cut into chunks
6 fresh dates, stones removed and cut into halves

1. Preheat oven to 200°C. Lightly grease 12 muffin tins.
2. Sift together flour, baking powder, baking soda and cinnamon into a bowl. Stir in sugar and make a well in the centre.
3. In another bowl lightly whisk together the melted butter, vanilla essence, egg and buttermilk. Stir in mashed banana and walnuts.
4. Fold banana mixture into dry ingredients and quickly stir to combine.
5. Gently fold in chunky banana pieces.
6. Spoon mixture into prepared muffin tins. Press half a fresh date into the top of each muffin. Bake for 12–15 minutes or until muffins spring back when lightly pressed.

Makes 12

Just a thought:
For a special treat when I have visitors, I sometimes split the muffins in half, fill with whipped cream and banana slices, replace the lid and dust with icing sugar.

baileys irish cream and coffee muffins

2 cups flour
4 teaspoons baking powder
$1/2$ cup soft brown sugar
4 teaspoons instant coffee powder
1 tablespoon boiling water
60 grams butter, melted
$1/4$ cup Baileys Irish Cream liqueur
$3/4$ cup milk
2 eggs
2 tablespoons chopped walnuts
icing sugar to dust top

1. Preheat oven to 200°C. Lightly grease 12 muffin tins.
2. Sift together flour and baking powder into a bowl, stir in sugar and make a well in the centre.
3. In a cup dissolve instant coffee in the boiling water.
4. In another bowl lightly whisk together the melted butter, Baileys, milk and eggs, and stir in instant coffee.
5. Fold Baileys mixture into dry ingredients and stir quickly to combine.
6. Spoon mixture into prepared muffin tins, sprinkle with chopped walnuts and bake for 12–15 minutes or until muffins spring back when lightly pressed.
7. Dust with icing sugar to serve.

Makes 12

Just a thought:
These are lovely made as mini muffins to serve at supper or to take as a plate to committee meetings or to bridge.

apple and fresh date muffins topped with amaretti biscuit crumble

2 cups flour
4 teaspoons baking powder
1/2 cup soft brown sugar
60 grams butter, melted
2 eggs
1 cup milk
1 cup stewed or canned apple
8 fresh dates, stones removed, chopped

amaretti biscuit crumble
6 amaretti biscuits
6 teaspoons butter, melted

1. Preheat oven to 200°C. Lightly grease 12 muffin tins.
2. Sift together flour and baking powder into a bowl, stir in sugar and make a well in the centre.
3. In another bowl lightly whisk together the melted butter, eggs and milk. Stir in stewed apples and dates.
4. Fold apple mixture into dry ingredients and stir quickly to combine.
5. Spoon mixture into prepared muffin tins.
6. To make crumble, place amaretti biscuits in a plastic bag and lightly crush with a rolling pin.
7. Sprinkle each muffin with the crushed amaretti biscuits and drizzle with melted butter.
8. Bake for 12–15 minutes or until muffins are golden and spring back when lightly pressed.

Makes 12

ginger beer muffins

1 cup ginger beer
3 tablespoons sugar
2 tablespoons golden syrup
20 grams butter
1 teaspoon baking soda
2 cups flour
2 teaspoons baking powder
75 grams crystallised ginger, thinly sliced
$\frac{1}{4}$ cup apple purée (sauce)

ginger cream topping (optional)
4 tablespoons whipped cream
12 slivers of crystallised ginger
icing sugar to dust on top

1. Preheat oven to 200°C. Lightly grease 12 muffin tins.
2. In a pot gently heat together the ginger beer, sugar, golden syrup and butter. When hot remove from heat and stir in baking soda. Allow mixture to cool.
3. Sift the flour and baking powder together into a bowl and make a well in the centre.
4. Stir crystallised ginger and apple purée into cooled ginger beer mixture. Fold into dry ingredients and stir quickly to combine.
5. Spoon mixture into prepared muffin tins and bake for 12–15 minutes or until muffins spring back when lightly pressed.
6. Ginger cream topping: Allow muffins to cool, then cut a slice off the top of the muffins and cut slice in half. Dab one teaspoon of cream in the centre of each muffin and stand the two cut pieces up in the cream to form 'fairy wings'. Place one piece of crystallised ginger in the centre of the 'wings' and dust with icing sugar.

Makes 12

coconut and raspberry muffins

2 cups flour
4 teaspoons baking powder
$^3/_4$ cup desiccated coconut
$^1/_4$ cup soft brown sugar
250 grams frozen raspberries, slightly thawed (reserve 12 for topping)
$^1/_4$ cup white sugar
1 teaspoon vanilla essence
60 grams butter, melted
2 eggs
1 cup milk
4 tablespoons shredded coconut for topping

raspberry couli
$1^1/_2$ cups frozen raspberries
$^1/_2$ cup sugar
2 tablespoons water

1. Preheat oven to 200°C. Lightly grease 12 muffin tins.
2. Sift together flour and baking powder into a bowl. Stir in coconut and soft brown sugar.
3. Place raspberries in a bowl and cover with white sugar.
4. In another bowl lightly whisk together the vanilla essence, melted butter, eggs and milk. Pour over raspberries.
5. Fold egg mixture into dry ingredients and stir quickly to combine.
6. Spoon mixture into prepared muffin tins, sprinkle with coconut shreds and press one raspberry into the centre of each muffin.
7. Bake for 12–15 minutes or until muffins spring back when lightly pressed. Serve drizzled with raspberry couli.
8. To prepare the raspberry couli, place frozen raspberries in a pot, add sugar and water and bring gently to the boil. Lower heat and simmer for 15 minutes,

stirring occasionally to prevent fruit from catching on the bottom of the pot. Allow coulis to cool, then pour into a sieve and using the back of a spoon press as much of the fruit through to form a smooth, seedless purée.

Makes 12

sugared grape muffins

500 grams grapes, seeded and cut in half (save 12 halves for decoration)
1/2 cup sugar
1 1/2 cups flour
3 teaspoons baking powder
1 teaspoon vanilla essence
juice and zest of 1 lemon
2 eggs

1. Preheat oven to 200°C. Lightly grease 12 muffin tins.
2. In a bowl toss together the grape halves and sugar. Reserve 12 sugared halves for decoration.
3. Sift together flour and baking powder into a bowl and make a well in the centre.
4. In another bowl lightly whisk together the vanilla essence, lemon juice, zest and eggs, and pour over grapes.
5. Fold grape mixture into dry ingredients and stir quickly to combine.
6. Spoon mixture into prepared muffin tins, press a sugared grape half into the top of each muffin and bake for 12–15 minutes or until muffins spring back when lightly pressed.

Makes 12

iced passionfruit muffins

2 cups flour
3 teaspoons baking powder
1/2 teaspoon baking soda
pulp of 6 passionfruit
60 grams butter, melted
2 eggs
1 cup buttermilk

passionfruit icing
1 cup icing sugar
pulp of 2 passionfruit
2 teaspoons butter, melted

1. Preheat oven to 200°C. Lightly grease 12 muffin tins.
2. Sift together flour, baking power and baking soda into a bowl and make a well in the centre.
3. In another bowl lightly whisk together the passionfruit pulp, melted butter, eggs and buttermilk.
4. Fold passionfruit mixture into dry ingredients and stir quickly to combine.
5. Spoon mixture into prepared muffin tins and bake for 12–15 minutes or until muffins spring back when lightly pressed. Allow muffins to cool for 5 minutes before icing.
6. To prepare the passionfruit icing, sift the icing sugar in a bowl and stir in the passionfruit pulp. Add melted butter and mix to a spreadable consistency, adding a small quantity of boiled water if necessary. Spread icing on top of each muffin.

Makes 12

walnut rice bubble muffins

2 cups flour
4 teaspoons baking powder
1/2 cup soft brown sugar
60 grams butter
1 tablespoon honey
2 eggs
3/4 cup milk
1 cup walnuts, chopped
1 1/2 cups rice bubbles

1. Preheat oven to 200°C. Lightly grease 12 muffin tins.
2. Sift together flour and baking powder into a bowl, stir in sugar and make a well in the centre.
3. In a pot melt together the butter and honey, and allow to cool.
4. In another bowl whisk together the melted butter and honey, eggs and milk. Stir in chopped walnuts.
5. Fold walnut mixture into dry ingredients and stir quickly to combine.
6. Gently fold in rice bubbles.
7. Spoon mixture into prepared muffin tins and bake for 12–15 minutes or until muffins spring back when lightly pressed.

Makes 12

wholemeal spiced apple afternoon tea muffins spread with apricot jam

1 cup wholemeal flour
1 cup white flour
4 teaspoons baking powder
1 teaspoon cinnamon
$1/4$ teaspoon nutmeg
$1/4$ teaspoon mixed spice
$1/4$ teaspoon ground ginger
pinch of salt
2 apples, peeled and grated
12 dried apricot halves, sliced
$1/2$ cup soft brown sugar
60 grams butter, melted
2 eggs
1 cup milk
12 pecan nuts
apricot jam to serve

cinnamon sugar topping
4 tablespoons sugar
1 teaspoon cinnamon

1. Preheat oven to 200°C. Lightly grease 12 muffin tins.
2. Sift together wholemeal and white flours, baking powder, cinnamon, nutmeg, mixed spice, ginger and salt into a bowl and make a well in the centre.
3. Place grated apples and apricots in a bowl and cover with the sugar.
4. In another bowl lightly whisk together the melted butter, eggs and milk, and pour over the apple mixture.
5. Fold apple mixture into dry ingredients and stir quickly to combine.
6. Spoon mixture into prepared muffin tins.

7. To make the cinnamon sugar topping, mix the sugar and cinnamon and sprinkle over muffins.
8. Press a pecan in the centre of each muffin.
9. Bake for 12–15 minutes or until muffins spring back when lightly pressed.
10. Serve muffins with apricot jam on the side.

Makes 12

Just a thought:
Home-made jams are delicious – try making Aunty Hilda's apricot jam on page 150.

caramel iced fruity muffins

16 dried dates, chopped
1/4 cup golden sultanas
1 teaspoon baking soda
1 1/4 cups boiling water
60 grams butter
3 tablespoons soft brown sugar
2 cups flour
2 teaspoons baking powder
1 teaspoon mixed spice

caramel icing

1/4 cup icing sugar
1 teaspoon golden syrup
2 teaspoons soft brown sugar
1/2 teaspoon vanilla essence
1 teaspoon butter, softened
2 teaspoons boiling water

1. Preheat oven to 200°C. Lightly grease 12 muffin tins.
2. Place dates, sultanas and baking soda in a large bowl and cover with the boiling water.
3. In a large pot melt the butter and sugar. Remove from heat and add the soaked dates, sultanas and water.
4. Sift together flour, baking powder and mixed spice into a bowl and make a well in the centre.
5. Fold the date mixture into dry ingredients and stir quickly to combine.
6. Spoon mixture into prepared muffin tins and bake for 12–15 minutes or until muffins spring back when lightly pressed. Allow muffins to cool for 5 minutes before removing to a cake rack for icing.
7. To make the caramel icing, mix the icing sugar, golden syrup, sugar, vanilla essence, butter and hot water in a bowl. Beat with a fork until smooth and spread a thin layer on top of each muffin.

Makes 12

sweet at heart jam muffins

2 cups flour
4 teaspoons baking powder
1/4 cup sugar
1/2 teaspoon vanilla essence
60 grams butter, melted
1 egg
1 cup milk
12 teaspoons strawberry conserve (refer page 150) or use commercial jam of your
        choice
6 fresh strawberries, cut in half (if in season)

1. Preheat oven to 200°C. Lightly grease 12 muffin tins.
2. Sift together flour and baking powder into a bowl, stir in sugar and make
    a well in the centre.
3. In another bowl lightly whisk together vanilla essence, melted butter,
    egg and milk.
4. Fold egg mixture into dry ingredients and stir quickly to combine.
5. Spoon one tablespoon of mixture into each of the prepared muffin tins.
    Place one teaspoon of conserve in the centre of each muffin and cover
    with the remaining mixture. If you have fresh strawberries, press one half
    into the top of the muffin mix.
6. Bake for 12–15 minutes or until muffins spring back when lightly
    pressed.

Makes 12

orange-infused date muffins spread with cream cheese icing

24 dates chopped
1 1/2 cups fresh orange juice
60 grams butter
2 tablespoons soft brown sugar
1 tablespoon grated orange zest
1 teaspoon baking soda
2 cups flour
2 teaspoons baking powder
1 teaspoon cinnamon

cream cheese icing

4 tablespoons cream cheese
2 tablespoons icing sugar
2 tablespoons orange juice
thin shreds of orange zest to decorate on top

1. Preheat oven to 200°C. Lightly grease 12 muffin tins.
2. Place dates and orange juice in a medium pot, bring to the boil and simmer gently for 5 minutes. Remove pot from heat and stir in butter, sugar, orange zest and baking soda. Set aside to cool.
3. Sift together flour, baking powder and cinnamon into a bowl and make a well in the centre.
4. Gently fold date mixture into dry ingredients and stir quickly to combine.
5. Spoon mixture into prepared muffin tins and bake for 12–15 minutes or until muffins spring back when lightly pressed. Allow muffins to cool for 5 minutes before removing to a cake rack in preparation for icing.
6. To prepare cream cheese icing, whisk the cream cheese, icing sugar and orange juice with a fork in a small bowl. Cut a small wedge out of the top of each muffin, place a teaspoon of cream cheese icing in the cut and top with the wedge. Decorate with a sprinkling of orange zest.

Makes 12

banoffee muffins with toasted almonds

12 gingernut biscuits
1 cup flour
2 teaspoons baking powder
1/4 cup soft brown sugar
2 bananas, peeled and chopped
1/2 cup caramel condensed milk
60 grams butter, melted
1 egg
1/4 cup milk
2 tablespoons sliced almonds

1. Preheat oven to 200°C. Lightly grease 12 muffin tins.
2. Place one gingernut, face down, in the bottom of each tin.
3. Sift together flour and baking powder into a bowl.
4. Stir in the sugar and make a well in the centre.
5. Place chopped bananas in a bowl and cover with caramel condensed milk.
6. In another bowl lightly whisk together the melted butter, egg and milk. Pour over the banana mixture.
7. Fold banana mixture into dry ingredients and stir quickly to combine.
8. Spoon mixture into prepared muffin tins and lightly sprinkle with sliced almonds.
9. Bake for 12–15 minutes or until muffins spring back when lightly pressed.

Makes 12

sugared carrot, walnut and date muffins

200 grams pitted dates, chopped
3 tablespoons soft brown sugar
1 tablespoon golden syrup
4 teaspoons olive or canola oil
1 teaspoon baking soda
1 1/4 cups boiling water
2 cups flour
2 teaspoons baking powder
2 teaspoons mixed spice
1 cup grated carrot
1/2 cup walnuts, chopped

sugared topping
2 tablespoons soft brown sugar
1 teaspoon mixed spice

1. Preheat oven to 200°C. Lightly grease 12 muffin tins.
2. In a bowl place dates, sugar, golden syrup, oil and baking soda, cover with boiling water and leave mixture to cool.
3. Sift together flour, baking powder and mixed spice into a bowl and make a well in the centre.
4. Stir the grated carrot and walnuts into the date mixture, then fold into the dry ingredients. Stir quickly to combine.
5. Spoon mixture into prepared muffin tins.
6. Mix together the topping ingredients and sprinkle over each muffin.
7. Bake for 12–15 minutes or until muffins spring back when lightly pressed.

Makes 12

glazed orange marmalade and pumpkin muffins

1½ cups flour
2 teaspoons baking powder
½ teaspoon baking soda
½ teaspoon salt
¼ cup sugar
60 grams butter, melted
2 eggs
¾ cup buttermilk
1½ cups pumpkin, cooked and mashed
½ cup orange marmalade

glaze
2 tablespoons orange marmalade

1. Preheat oven to 200°C. Lightly grease 12 muffin tins.
2. Sift together flour, baking powder, baking soda and salt into a bowl, stir in sugar and make a well in the centre.
3. In another bowl whisk together melted butter, eggs and buttermilk. Stir in mashed pumpkin and orange marmalade.
4. Fold the pumpkin mixture into the dry ingredients and stir quickly to combine.
5. Spoon mixture into prepared muffin tins and bake for 12–15 minutes or until muffins spring back when lightly pressed. Allow muffins to cool before glazing.
6. To glaze, heat the orange marmalade until slightly runny and using a pastry brush paint the top of each muffin.
7. Serve warm.

Makes 12

sour cream, pineapple and passionfruit muffins

5 dried pineapple rings, cut into small pieces
pulp of 6 passionfruit
$^1/_2$ cup sugar
$^1/_2$ cup sour cream
2 cups flour
4 teaspoons baking powder
2 eggs
1 cup milk
1 tablespoon icing sugar

1. Preheat oven to 200°C. Lightly grease 12 muffin tins.
2. In a bowl combine the pineapple pieces, passionfruit pulp, sugar and sour cream.
3. Sift together flour and baking powder into a bowl and make a well in the centre.
4. In another bowl lightly whisk together the eggs and milk, and pour over pineapple mixture.
5. Fold pineapple mixture into dry ingredients and stir quickly to combine.
6. Spoon mixture into prepared muffin tins and bake for 12–15 minutes or until muffins spring back when lightly pressed.
7. Serve dusted with icing sugar.

Makes 12

apricot and chocolate chip muffins

2 cups flour
4 teaspoons baking powder
2 tablespoons cocoa
$1/4$ cup soft brown sugar
$1/4$ cup white sugar
1 teaspoon vanilla essence
60 grams butter, melted
2 eggs
1 cup milk
120 grams chocolate buttons or morsels, chopped
250 grams apricot halves (reserve 12 halves for topping and chop
   rest into small pieces)
6 teaspoons icing sugar mixed with 1 teaspoon cocoa to dust

1. Preheat oven to 200°C. Lightly grease 12 muffin tins.
2. Sift together flour, baking powder and cocoa into a bowl. Stir in brown and white sugars and make a well in the centre.
3. In another bowl lightly whisk together the vanilla essence, melted butter, eggs and milk. Stir in the chocolate buttons and apricot halves.
4. Fold egg mixture into dry ingredients and stir quickly to combine.
5. Spoon mixture into prepared muffin tins. Press one apricot half on top of each muffin and bake for 12–15 minutes or until muffins spring back when lightly pressed.
6. Lightly dust with cocoa icing sugar.

Makes 12

strawberry meringue muffins with fresh berries on the side

coconut meringue topping

1 egg white
3/4 cup sugar
2 tablespoons boiling water

1 teaspoon vinegar
1 teaspoon baking powder
3/4 cup desiccated coconut

muffins

2 cups flour
4 teaspoons baking powder
1/2 cup ground almonds
1/2 cup sugar

60 grams butter, melted
2 eggs
1 cup milk
4 tablespoons strawberry jam

1. To make topping, place egg white in a bowl, add sugar, boiling water and vinegar and beat until very stiff. Stir in baking powder and coconut. Set aside.
2. Preheat oven to 180°C. Lightly grease 12 muffin tins.
3. Sift together flour and baking powder into a bowl. Stir in ground almonds and sugar, and make a well in the centre.
4. In another bowl lightly whisk together melted butter, eggs and milk and fold into dry ingredients. Stir quickly to combine.
5. Spoon mixture into prepared muffin tins and top each with one teaspoon of strawberry jam.
6. Cover top of each muffin with coconut meringue mixture and bake for 14–16 minutes. Allow muffins to cool for 10 minutes before carefully removing to a cake rack. Serve with fresh strawberries.

Makes 12

peanut brittle muffins

2 cups flour
4 teaspoons baking powder
1/2 cup soft brown sugar
60 grams butter
6 tablespoons crunchy peanut butter
6 tablespoons white sugar
3 tablespoons liquid honey
1/2 cup peanuts, chopped
2 eggs
1/2 cup milk
1 apple, peeled and chopped

1. Preheat oven to 200°C. Lightly grease 12 muffin tins.
2. Sift together flour and baking powder into a bowl, stir in brown sugar and make a well in the centre.
3. In a pot gently heat together butter, peanut butter, white sugar, liquid honey and chopped peanuts. Allow to cool.
4. In another bowl lightly whisk together eggs and milk, then stir in chopped apple.
5. Fold peanut mixture and egg mixture into dry ingredients and stir quickly to combine.
6. Spoon mixture into prepared muffin tins and bake for 12–15 minutes or until muffins spring back when lightly pressed.

Makes 12

prunes in port muffins with whipped cinnamon cream

36 chopped prunes
1/2 cup port
2 cups flour
4 teaspoons baking powder
1 teaspoon cinnamon
1/2 cup soft brown sugar
60 grams butter, melted
2 eggs
1 cup milk
zest of 1 lemon
12 extra prunes for top

cinnamon cream
3/4 cup whipped cream
1 teaspoon icing sugar
1 teaspoon cinnamon

1. Place prunes in a bowl, cover with port and leave to soak overnight.
2. Preheat oven to 200°C. Lightly grease 12 muffin tins.
3. Sift flour, baking powder and cinnamon into a bowl. Stir in sugar and make a well in centre.
4. In another bowl lightly whisk together the melted butter, eggs, milk and lemon zest, and pour over the prune mixture.
5. Fold prune mixture into dry ingredients and stir quickly to combine.
6. Spoon mixture into prepared muffin tins. Press one prune into each muffin and bake for 12–15 minutes or until muffins spring back when lightly pressed.
7. To prepare cinnamon cream, combine the cream and icing sugar in a small bowl. Serve spooned on the side of the warm muffins and dust cream with cinnamon.

Makes 12

a walk in the black forest muffins

12 chocolate wheaten biscuits, medium-sized
6 teaspoons strawberry conserve (refer page 150)
2 cups flour
4 teaspoons baking powder
4 tablespoons cocoa
3/4 cup sugar
60 grams butter, melted
2 eggs
1 cup milk
24 pitted cherries (I used cherries packed in syrup in a jar)
20 chocolate melts, chopped

1. Preheat oven to 200°C. Lightly grease 12 muffin tins.
2. Place one chocolate wheaten biscuit, chocolate-side up, in the bottom of each tin.
3. Spoon half a teaspoon of jam on top of each biscuit.
4. Sift together flour, baking powder and cocoa into a bowl, stir in sugar and make a well in the centre.
5. In another bowl lightly whisk together melted butter, eggs and milk.
6. Stir in cherries and chocolate melts.
7. Fold cherry mixture into dry ingredients and stir quickly to combine.
8. Spoon mixture into prepared muffin tins and bake for 12–15 minutes or until muffins spring back when lightly pressed.

Makes 12

coconut rough muffins

1 cup flour
4 teaspoons baking powder
1 tablespoon cocoa
1 cup coconut
1/2 cup sugar
60 grams butter, melted
1 egg
1 cup milk
1/2 teaspoon coconut essence

coconut rough topping

3/4 cup icing sugar
1/2 cup coconut
1 teaspoon cocoa

1 tablespoon butter
vanilla essence
2 teaspoons hot water

1. Preheat oven to 200°C. Lightly grease 12 muffin tins.
2. Sift together flour, baking powder and cocoa into a bowl.
3. Stir in the coconut and sugar, and make a well in the centre.
4. In another bowl lightly whisk together the melted butter, egg, milk and coconut essence.
5. Fold egg mixture into dry ingredients and stir quickly to combine.
6. Spoon mixture into prepared muffin tins and bake for 12–15 minutes or until muffins spring back when lightly pressed.
7. To make the coconut rough topping, mix together topping ingredients in a small pot. Gently warm on element and stir until butter melts into ingredients. Remove from heat and allow to cool slightly before icing muffins.

Makes 12

crystallised ginger and pineapple muffins

2 cups flour
2 teaspoons baking powder
3 teaspoons ground ginger
$1/4$ teaspoon salt
$1/4$ cup soft brown sugar
60 grams butter
4 tablespoons golden syrup
$1/2$ teaspoon baking soda
1 egg
$1/2$ cup buttermilk
75 grams crystallised ginger, chopped
75 grams crystallised pineapple, chopped

1. Preheat oven to 200°C. Lightly grease 12 muffin tins.
2. Sift together flour, baking powder, ground ginger and salt into a bowl.
3. Stir in sugar and make a well in the centre.
4. In a small pot melt together the butter and golden syrup. Remove from heat and stir in baking soda.
5. In another bowl lightly whisk together the egg and buttermilk. Stir in the crystallised ginger and pineapple.
6. Fold crystallised fruit mixture into dry ingredients and stir quickly to combine.
7. Spoon mixture into prepared muffin tins and bake for 12–15 minutes or until muffins spring back when lightly pressed.

Makes 12

'lest we forget' anzac muffins

1 cup flour
2 teaspoons baking powder
$^1/_2$ teaspoon baking soda
1 cup desiccated coconut
1 cup rolled oats
$^1/_2$ cup soft brown sugar
60 grams butter
1 tablespoon golden syrup
1 cup buttermilk
2 eggs

1. Preheat oven to 200°C. Lightly grease 12 muffin tins.
2. Sift together flour, baking powder and baking soda into a bowl.
3. Stir in the coconut, rolled oats and sugar and make a well in the centre.
4. In a small pot melt together the butter and golden syrup.
5. In another bowl lightly whisk together the buttermilk and eggs. Stir in the melted butter and golden syrup.
6. Fold the egg mixture into the dry ingredients and stir quickly to combine.
7. Spoon mixture into prepared muffin tins and bake for 12–15 minutes or until muffins spring back when lightly pressed.

Makes 12

sweet potato, pecan and maple syrup muffins

1 cup sweet potato, cooked and mashed
2 cups flour
4 teaspoons baking powder
1 teaspoon mixed spice
1/4 cup soft brown sugar
3/4 cup pecans, chopped
60 grams butter
1/2 cup maple syrup
1 teaspoon vanilla essence
2 eggs
1 cup milk
12 teaspoons maple syrup for topping

1. Preheat oven to 200°C. Lightly grease 12 muffin tins.
2. Place mashed sweet potato in a large bowl. Stir in sifted flour, baking powder and mixed spice.
3. Stir in sugar and chopped pecans.
4. In a small pot gently heat together the butter and maple syrup. Remove from heat and allow to cool slightly.
5. In another bowl whisk together the vanilla essence, eggs and milk. Combine with the melted butter and maple syrup.
6. Fold the egg mixture into the dry ingredients and stir quickly to combine.
7. Spoon mixture into prepared muffin tins and bake for 12–15 minutes or until muffins spring back when lightly pressed.
8. Serve each muffin drizzled with one teaspoon of maple syrup.

Makes 12

chocolate brazil muffins

2 cups flour
4 teaspoons baking powder
2 tablespoons cocoa
$1/4$ cup soft brown sugar
$1/4$ cup white sugar
60 grams butter, melted
2 eggs
1 cup milk
1 teaspoon vanilla essence
120 grams chocolate buttons, chopped
1 cup Brazil nuts, roughly chopped
6 extra Brazil nuts, finely chopped, for topping

1. Preheat oven to 200°C. Lightly grease 12 muffin tins.
2. Sift together flour, baking powder and cocoa into a bowl. Stir in brown and white sugars and make a well in the centre.
3. In another bowl whisk together melted butter, eggs, milk and vanilla essence. Stir in chocolate buttons and Brazil nuts.
4. Fold chocolate mixture into dry ingredients and stir quickly to combine.
5. Spoon mixture into prepared muffin tins and sprinkle chopped Brazil nuts on top.
6. Bake for 12–15 minutes or until muffins spring back when lightly pressed.

Makes 12

sticky apricot-glazed madeira muffins

2 cups flour
4 teaspoons baking powder
1/2 cup ground almonds
3/4 cup sugar
60 grams butter, melted
2 eggs
zest and juice of 1 orange (approx. 1/2 cup juice)
1/2 cup milk

sticky apricot glaze
2 tablespoons apricot jam
1 teaspoon water

1. Preheat oven to 200°C. Lightly grease 12 muffin tins.
2. Sift together flour and baking powder into a bowl. Stir in ground almonds and sugar and make a well in the centre.
3. In another bowl lightly whisk together melted butter, eggs, zest and juice of orange and milk.
4. Fold egg mixture into dry ingredients and stir quickly to combine.
5. Spoon mixture into prepared muffin tins and bake for 12–15 minutes or until muffins spring back when lightly pressed.
6. Allow muffins to cool for 5 minutes in the tin before removing to a cake rack to be glazed.
7. To make sticky apricot glaze, gently heat apricot jam and water in a small pot. Lightly brush muffins with glaze and allow to cool.

Makes 12

lemon and honey wholemeal muffins

1 1/2 cups sultanas
juice of 1 lemon
1 tablespoon lemon zest
1 cup wholemeal flour
1 cup white flour
3 teaspoons baking powder
1/2 teaspoon baking soda
1 teaspoon ground ginger
1/4 teaspoon salt
60 grams butter, melted
1/2 cup liquid honey
1 egg
3/4 cup milk

1. Preheat oven to 200°C. Lightly grease 12 muffin tins.
2. Place sultanas, lemon juice and zest in a small bowl and leave to soak for 30 minutes.
3. Sift wholemeal flour, white flour, baking powder, baking soda, ginger and salt into a bowl and make a well in the centre.
4. In another bowl lightly whisk together the melted butter, honey, egg and milk, and pour into sultana mixture.
5. Fold sultana mixture into dry ingredients and stir quickly to combine.
6. Spoon mixture into prepared muffin tins and bake for 12–15 minutes or until muffins spring back when lightly pressed.

Makes 12

jamaican rum, date and banana muffins

1 cup dates, chopped
60 grams butter
1/4 cup soft brown sugar
3 tablespoons golden syrup
1/4 cup freshly squeezed orange juice
zest of 1/2 an orange
1/2 cup Jamaican rum
1 egg
2 bananas, peeled and cut into small chunks
2 cups flour
4 teaspoons baking powder
1 teaspoon mixed spice

1. Preheat oven to 200°C. Lightly grease 12 muffin tins.
2. In a pot gently heat together the dates, butter, sugar, golden syrup, orange juice and zest and rum. Simmer for a few minutes, then allow to cool.
3. In another bowl lightly whisk egg, then stir in banana chunks. Pour into rum mixture.
4. Sift together flour, baking powder and mixed spice into a bowl and make a well in the centre.
5. Fold rum mixture into dry ingredients and stir quickly to combine.
6. Spoon mixture into prepared muffin tins and bake for 12–15 minutes or until muffins spring back when lightly pressed.

Makes 12

plumped orange-soaked craisin muffins

1 cup craisins (dried cranberries, available in supermarkets)
1 cup orange juice, fresh or packaged
60 grams butter
1/2 cup sugar
2 cups flour
4 teaspoons baking powder
2 eggs
icing sugar for dusting top

1. Preheat oven to 200°C. Lightly grease 12 muffin tins.
2. Place craisins and orange juice in a pot and simmer for 5 minutes. Add butter and remove from heat. Allow to cool slightly, then stir in sugar.
3. Sift together flour and baking powder into a bowl and make a well in the centre.
4. In another bowl lightly whisk eggs and pour over the cooled craisin mixture.
5. Fold craisin mixture into dry ingredients and stir quickly to combine.
6. Spoon mixture into prepared muffin tins and bake for 12–15 minutes or until muffins spring back when lightly pressed.
7. Serve warm dusted with icing sugar.

Makes 12

macadamia nuts, oats and caramel muffins

1½ cups flour
4 teaspoons baking powder
½ cup rolled oats
¼ cup demerara sugar
½ cup macadamia nuts, chopped
60 grams butter, melted
1 teaspoon vanilla essence
1 egg
½ cup caramel or plain condensed milk
½ cup milk
2 tablespoons macadamia nuts, chopped, for top

1. Preheat oven to 200°C. Lightly grease 12 muffin tins.
2. Sift together flour and baking powder into a bowl and make a well in the centre.
3. Stir in the rolled oats, sugar and chopped macadamia nuts.
4. In another bowl lightly whisk together the melted butter, vanilla essence, egg, condensed milk and milk.
5. Fold egg mixture into dry ingredients and stir quickly to combine.
6. Spoon mixture into prepared muffin tins, sprinkle with chopped macadamia nuts and bake for 12–15 minutes or until muffins spring back when lightly pressed.

Makes 12

lemon curd and walnut muffins with a sweet syrup glaze

2 cups flour
4 teaspoons baking powder
pinch of salt
$1/2$ cup sugar
60 grams butter, melted
2 eggs
$1^{1}/_2$ cups milk
1 tablespoon lemon zest
2 tablespoons chopped walnuts
12 teaspoons lemon curd

sweet syrup glaze
$1/4$ cup lemon juice
3 tablespoons sugar

1. Preheat oven to 200°C. Lightly grease 12 muffin tins.
2. Sift together flour, baking powder and salt into a bowl, stir in sugar and make a well in the centre.
3. In another bowl lightly whisk together the melted butter, eggs and milk. Stir in the lemon zest and chopped walnuts.
4. Fold egg mixture into dry ingredients and stir quickly to combine.
5. Spoon one tablespoon of mixture into each prepared muffin tin.
6. Spoon one teaspoon of lemon curd into the centre of each muffin and top with the remaining mixture.
7. Bake for 12–15 minutes or until muffins spring back when lightly pressed.
8. To prepare sweet syrup glaze, place lemon juice and sugar in a small pot, bring to the boil and gently simmer for 5 minutes or until syrup thickens.

9. Allow muffins to cool before pouring lemon syrup over each muffin.
   (I like to pierce the muffins with a skewer to allow the syrup to sink in.)

Makes 12

Just a thought:
I have only recently discovered lemon curd and have included my recipe on page 151. It's wonderful on a piece of toast in the afternoon so that it doesn't go to waste.

ginger, apricot and date muffins

2 cups flour
4 teaspoons baking powder
1 teaspoon ground ginger
$^1/_2$ cup sugar
60 grams butter, melted
2 eggs
$^3/_4$ cup milk
$^1/_2$ cup dates, chopped
$^1/_2$ cup dried apricots, chopped
2 tablespoons crystallised ginger, chopped
$1^1/_2$ cups rice bubbles

1. Preheat oven to 200°C. Lightly grease 12 muffin tins.
2. Sift together flour, baking powder and ground ginger into a bowl, stir in sugar and make a well in the centre.
3. In another bowl lightly whisk together melted butter, eggs and milk. Stir in dates, dried apricots and crystallised ginger.
4. Fold date mixture into dry ingredients and stir quickly to combine.
5. Gently fold in rice bubbles.
6. Spoon mixture into prepared muffin tins and bake for 12–15 minutes or until muffins spring back when lightly pressed.

Makes 12

kiwifruit muffins glazed with lime marmalade

2 cups flour
4 teaspoons baking powder
2 tablespoons custard powder
1 cup kiwifruit, peeled and chopped into small chunks
3/4 cup sugar
60 grams butter, melted
2 eggs
1 cup milk
2 tablespoons lime marmalade for glaze

1. Preheat oven to 200°C. Lightly grease 12 muffin tins.
2. Sift together flour, baking powder and custard powder into a bowl and make a well in the centre.
3. Place chopped kiwifruit in another bowl and sprinkle with the sugar.
4. In another bowl whisk together the melted butter, eggs and milk, and pour over the kiwifruit mixture.
5. Fold the kiwifruit mixture into dry ingredients and stir quickly to combine.
6. Spoon mixture into prepared muffin tins and bake for 12–15 minutes or until muffins spring back when lightly pressed.
7. Allow muffins to cool.
8. Warm the marmalade in a small pot and using a pastry brush glaze the top of each muffin.

Makes 12

yoghurt, banana and raisin bran muffins

2 cups flour
4 teaspoons baking powder
1 cup baker's bran flakes
2 tablespoons soft brown sugar
60 grams butter, melted
2 tablespoons golden syrup
1 banana, mashed
3/4 cup raisins
3/4 cup fruit yoghurt
1/2 cup milk
1 teaspoon baking soda

cinnamon sugar topping (optional)
1 tablespoon soft brown sugar
1 tablespoon white sugar
1 teaspoon cinnamon

1. Preheat oven to 200°C. Lightly grease 12 muffin tins.
2. Sift together flour and baking powder into a bowl. Stir in bran flakes and sugar and make a well in the centre.
3. In a pot gently heat together the butter and golden syrup. When butter has melted, remove pot from the heat and stir in mashed banana, raisins, yoghurt, milk and baking soda.
4. Fold banana mixture into dry ingredients and stir quickly to combine.
5. To make cinnamon sugar topping, combine topping ingredients.
6. Spoon muffin mixture into prepared muffin tins. Sprinkle each muffin with cinnamon sugar and bake for 12–15 minutes or until muffins spring back when lightly pressed.

Makes 12

gin and tonic with a twist of lemon muffins

1 cup raisins
1/2 cup gin
2 cups flour
4 teaspoons baking powder
1/2 cup sugar
60 grams butter, melted
juice and zest of 1/2 a lemon
3/4 cup tonic water

twist of lemon topping
3 tablespoons sugar
6 slices lemon, cut into halves (12 pieces)

1. Place raisins and gin in a bowl, cover and soak overnight.
2. Preheat oven to 200°C. Lightly grease 12 muffin tins.
3. Sift together flour, baking powder and sugar into a bowl and make a well in the centre.
4. In another bowl whisk together the melted butter, lemon juice and zest and tonic water, and pour over raisin and gin mixture.
5. Fold raisin mixture into dry ingredients and stir quickly to combine.
6. Spoon mixture into prepared muffin tins.
7. To make twist of lemon topping, sprinkle sugar onto a small flat plate and press each of the lemon half slices into the sugar to lightly coat on each side. Twist the lemon slice and press into the top of each muffin.
8. Bake for 12–15 minutes or until muffins spring back when lightly pressed.

Makes 12

afternoon tea on the lawn with glacé cherry muffins

2 cups flour
3 teaspoons baking powder
1 teaspoon baking soda
$^1/_2$ cup sugar
1 teaspoon vanilla essence
60 grams butter, melted
2 eggs
1 cup buttermilk
$^1/_2$ cup red glacé cherries
$^1/_2$ cup green glacé cherries
12 glacé cherries for the top
icing sugar to dust

1. Preheat oven to 200°C. Lightly grease 12 muffin tins.
2. Sift together flour, baking powder and baking soda into a bowl, stir in sugar and make a well in the centre.
3. In another bowl lightly whisk together the vanilla essence, melted butter, eggs and buttermilk. Stir in the red and green glacé cherries.
4. Fold cherry mixture into dry ingredients and stir quickly to combine.
5. Spoon mixture into prepared muffin tins. Press a glacé cherry into the centre of each muffin and bake for 12–15 minutes or until muffins spring back when lightly pressed. Allow muffins to cool before dusting with icing sugar.

Makes 12

orange, cardamom pear muffins with a macaroon crumble

1½ cups dried pear pieces, chopped
½ cup fresh orange juice
zest of 1 orange
6 tablespoons honey
60 grams butter
1 teaspoon baking soda
2 cups flour
4 teaspoons baking powder
1 teaspoon ground cardamom
½ cup sugar
2 eggs
¼ cup milk

macaroon crumble

¼ cup ground almonds
¼ cup caster sugar

3 tablespoons coconut
4 teaspoons butter

1. Preheat oven to 200°C. Lightly grease 12 muffin tins.
2. In a small pot mix together pears, orange juice and zest and honey. Gently heat and simmer for a few minutes until pears slightly soften.
3. Add butter and when melted remove from heat and stir in baking soda. Put to one side to allow to slightly cool.
4. Sift together flour, baking powder and ground cardamom into a bowl, stir in sugar and make a well in the centre.
5. In another bowl lightly whisk together the eggs and milk and pour over pear mixture.
6. Fold pear mixture into dry ingredients and stir quickly to combine.
7. Spoon mixture into prepared muffin tins.

8. To make macaroon crumble, combine ground almonds, sugar and coconut in a bowl, and rub in butter to form a crumble. Sprinkle on top of the muffins.
9. Bake for 12–15 minutes or until crumble is lightly golden and muffins spring back when lightly pressed.

Makes 12

and then along came the blueberry muffins

2 cups flour
2 teaspoons baking powder
1/2 teaspoon baking soda
pinch of salt
1/2 cup soft brown sugar
60 grams butter
1 egg
1/2 cup milk
1/4 cup natural yoghurt
2 cups blueberries, fresh or frozen

1. Preheat oven to 200°C. Lightly grease 12 muffin tins.
2. Sift together flour, baking powder, baking soda and salt into a large bowl, stir in sugar and make a well in the centre.
3. Melt butter in a small pot and allow to cool.
4. In another bowl lightly whisk together the egg, milk, yoghurt and melted butter. Stir into dry ingredients with blueberries.
5. Spoon mixture evenly into prepared muffin tins.
6. Bake for 12–15 minutes or until muffins spring back when lightly pressed.

Makes 12

fruits of the forest muffins with a hazelnut streusel

2 cups frozen mixed berries, slightly thawed
$1/4$ cup white sugar
2 cups flour
2 teaspoons baking powder
1 teaspoon baking soda
$1/4$ cup soft brown sugar
60 grams butter, melted
2 eggs
1 cup buttermilk
1 teaspoon vanilla essence

hazelnut streusel
$1/4$ cup sugar
$1/4$ cup flour
2 tablespoons chopped hazelnuts
30 grams butter, melted

1. Preheat oven to 200°C. Lightly grease 12 muffin tins.
2. Place mixed berries in a bowl and cover with white sugar.
3. To make hazelnut streusel, combine sugar, flour and chopped hazelnuts in a bowl, then stir in melted butter. Set aside.
4. Sift together flour, baking powder and baking soda into a bowl, stir in soft brown sugar and make a well in the centre.
5. In another bowl lightly whisk together melted butter, eggs, buttermilk and vanilla essence. Add to berry mixture.
6. Fold berry mixture into dry ingredients and stir quickly to combine.
7. Spoon mixture into prepared muffin tins. Top with hazelnut streusel and bake for 12–15 minutes or until muffins spring back when lightly pressed.

Makes 12

sticky english gingerbread muffins

2 cups flour
2 teaspoons baking powder
1 teaspoon baking soda
$1/4$ teaspoon salt
2 teaspoons ground ginger
$1/2$ teaspoon cinnamon
$1/2$ teaspoon mixed spice
$1/4$ cup soft brown sugar
60 grams butter
$1/4$ cup golden syrup
1 egg
1 cup milk

1. Preheat oven to 200°C. Lightly grease 12 muffin tins.
2. Sift together flour, baking powder, baking soda, salt, ginger, cinnamon and mixed spice into a bowl, stir in sugar and make a well in the centre.
3. In a pot gently heat together the butter and golden syrup.
4. In another bowl lightly whisk together egg and milk, and pour into melted butter and golden syrup.
5. Fold egg mixture into dry ingredients and stir quickly to combine.
6. Spoon mixture into prepared muffin tins and bake for 12–15 minutes or until muffins spring back when lightly pressed.

Makes 12

double espresso muffins

2 cups flour
4 teaspoons baking powder
$\frac{1}{2}$ cup sugar
$\frac{1}{2}$ cup pecans, chopped
1 tablespoon instant coffee
1 tablespoon boiling water
60 grams butter, melted
2 eggs
1 cup milk

espresso glaze
$\frac{1}{2}$ cup icing sugar
1 teaspoon instant coffee
1–2 teaspoons boiling water

1. Preheat oven to 200°C. Lightly grease 12 muffin tins.
2. Sift together flour and baking powder into a bowl, stir in the sugar and pecans and make a well in the centre.
3. In another bowl dissolve the coffee in the boiling water and allow to cool.
4. Add the coffee to the melted butter, eggs and milk, and lightly whisk together.
5. Fold egg mixture into dry ingredients and stir quickly to combine.
6. Spoon mixture into prepared muffin tins and bake for 12–15 minutes or until muffins spring back when lightly pressed.
7. To make espresso glaze, combine icing sugar and coffee in a bowl and add enough boiling water to make a spreadable consistency. Drizzle over the top of each muffin.

Makes 12

cinnamon muffins topped with apple dipped in warmed manuka honey

6 tablespoons manuka honey
1 apple, cored, skin left on and cut into thin slices
2 cups flour
3 teaspoons baking powder
1 teaspoon baking soda
2 teaspoons cinnamon
1 cup demerara sugar
60 grams butter, melted
2 eggs
1 cup buttermilk

1. Preheat oven to 200°C. Lightly grease 12 muffin tins.
2. In a pot gently warm the manuka honey, then dip the apple slices to coat. Put to one side to cool.
3. Sift together flour, baking powder, baking soda and cinnamon into a bowl, stir in sugar and make a well in the centre.
4. In another bowl lightly whisk together the melted butter, eggs and buttermilk.
5. Fold egg mixture into dry ingredients and stir quickly to combine.
6. Spoon mixture into prepared muffin tins. Fan honey-dipped apple slices on top and bake for 12–15 minutes or until muffins spring back when lightly pressed.

Makes 12

toasted muesli muffins

2 tablespoons sesame seeds
2 tablespoons sunflower seeds
1/4 cup desiccated coconut
1/2 cup rolled oats
30 grams butter
30 grams crunchy peanut butter
1/4 cup liquid honey
1 cup flour
4 teaspoons baking powder
1/2 cup puffed wheat
1/4 cup soft brown sugar
2 eggs
3/4 cup milk
1 cup mixed dried fruit (e.g. raisins apricots, prunes and figs), chopped
1 tablespoon sesame seeds to sprinkle on top

1. Preheat oven to 200°C. Lightly grease 12 muffin tins.
2. Place sesame seeds, sunflower seeds, coconut and rolled oats in a non-stick pan and toss on a low heat to lightly toast. Remove from heat and allow to cool.
3. In a pot heat together the butter, peanut butter and liquid honey. Remove from heat and allow to cool.
4. Sift together flour and baking powder into a bowl. Stir in toasted seed mixture, puffed wheat and sugar, and make a well in the centre.
5. In another bowl lightly whisk together the eggs and milk. Stir in the mixed dried fruit and the cooled butter mixture.
6. Fold fruit mixture into dry ingredients and stir quickly to combine.
7. Spoon mixture into prepared muffin tins, sprinkle with sesame seeds and bake for 12–15 minutes or until muffins spring back when lightly pressed.

Makes 12

almond peach melba muffins

2 cups flour
3 teaspoons baking powder
1 teaspoon baking soda
$1/4$ cup sugar
60 grams butter, melted
2 eggs
1 cup milk
$1/4$ teaspoon almond essence
1 cup canned peaches, drained and chopped
$1/4$ cup raspberry jam
$1/4$ cup sliced almonds for topping

1. Preheat oven to 200°C. Lightly grease 12 muffin tins.
2. Sift together flour, baking powder and baking soda into a bowl, stir in sugar and make a well in the centre.
3. In another bowl lightly whisk together melted butter, eggs, milk and almond essence.
4. Stir in chopped peaches.
5. Fold peach mixture into dry ingredients and stir quickly to combine.
6. Spoon one tablespoon of mixture into prepared muffin tins. Top with one teaspoon raspberry jam and cover with remaining mixture. Use a fork to ripple jam through each muffin.
7. Sprinkle the top of each muffin with sliced almonds.
8. Bake muffins for 12–15 minutes or until muffins spring back when lightly pressed.

Makes 12

danish apple muffins

2 apples (Granny Smith are excellent)
$^2/_3$ cup sugar
$1^1/_2$ cups flour
2 teaspoons baking powder
$^1/_2$ teaspoon baking soda
$^1/_2$ teaspoon mixed spice
$^1/_2$ teaspoon nutmeg
$^1/_2$ teaspoon cinnamon
$^1/_2$ cup sultanas
60 grams butter, melted
$^1/_2$ cup milk
1 egg
icing sugar for dusting

1. Preheat oven to 200°C. Lightly grease 12 muffin tins.
2. Peel and slice apples, place in a bowl and cover with sugar.
3. Sift together flour, baking powder, baking soda, mixed spice, nutmeg and cinnamon into a bowl, add sultanas and make a well in the centre.
4. In another bowl lightly whisk together the melted butter, milk and egg. Stir in the apple mixture.
5. Fold apple mixture into dry ingredients and stir quickly to combine.
6. Spoon mixture into prepared muffin tins and bake for 12–15 minutes or until muffins spring back when lightly pressed.
7. Serve muffins warm dusted with icing sugar.

Makes 12

iced ginger crunch muffins

2 cups flour
4 teaspoons baking powder
1/2 cup sugar
1 cup cornflakes, lightly crushed (not into powder)
2 tablespoons crystallised ginger, finely chopped
60 grams butter, melted
1 cup milk

ginger crunch icing
1 cup icing sugar
2 teaspoons butter
2 teaspoons ground ginger
4 teaspoons boiling water
2 crushed gingernuts (optional)

1. Preheat oven to 200°C. Lightly grease 12 muffin tins.
2. Sift together flour and baking powder into a bowl, stir in sugar, cornflakes and crystallised ginger, and make a well in the centre.
3. In another bowl whisk together the melted butter and milk. Fold into the dry ingredients and stir quickly to combine.
4. Spoon mixture into prepared tins and bake for 12–15 minutes or until muffins spring back when lightly pressed. Allow muffins to cool before icing.
5. To make the ginger crunch icing, beat together the icing sugar, butter and ground ginger in a small bowl. Add the boiling water slowly until mixture comes together but isn't too runny. Spread icing over the top of each muffin and sprinkle with crushed gingernuts.

Makes 12

sultana bran muffins spread with honeycomb butter

1 cup baker's bran flakes
$^3/_4$ cup buttermilk
1 tablespoon golden syrup
1 cup sultanas
1 egg, lightly beaten
$^3/_4$ cup flour
2 teaspoons baking powder
1 teaspoon baking soda
$^1/_2$ teaspoon cinnamon
$^1/_2$ teaspoon ground ginger
$^1/_4$ teaspoon salt
$^1/_3$ cup sugar

1. Preheat oven to 200°C. Lightly grease 10–12 muffin tins.
2. In a bowl mix together bran, buttermilk, golden syrup and sultanas. Leave to soak for 5 minutes, then stir in beaten egg.
3. Sift together flour, baking powder, baking soda, cinnamon, ground ginger and salt into a bowl, stir in sugar and make a well in the centre.
4. Fold bran mixture into dry ingredients and stir quickly to combine.
5. Spoon mixture into prepared muffin tins and bake for 12–15 minutes or until muffins spring back when lightly pressed.
6. Serve muffins warm spread with honeycomb butter (refer page 154).

Makes 10–12

rum-soaked raisin muffins

1 cup seedless raisins
2 tablespoons dark rum
1/4 cup soft brown sugar
1 tablespoon golden syrup
60 grams butter
1 cup apple and blackcurrant juice
2 teaspoons baking soda
2 cups flour
2 teaspoons baking powder
1 teaspoon cinnamon

1. Place raisins and rum in a bowl and leave to soak for 30 minutes or overnight.
2. Preheat oven to 200°C. Lightly grease 12 muffin tins.
3. In a small pot heat together the sugar, golden syrup, butter and apple and blackcurrant juice. When warm, dissolve the baking soda in the mixture. Stir into the bowl of raisins.
4. Sift together flour, baking powder and cinnamon into a bowl and make a well in the centre.
5. Fold the raisin mixture into the dry ingredients and stir quickly to combine.
6. Spoon mixture into prepared muffin tins and bake for 12–15 minutes or until muffins spring back when lightly pressed.

Makes 12

spiced prune and walnut muffins

24 prunes, chopped
1/2 cup soft brown sugar
1/4 teaspoon ground cloves
1/2 teaspoon ground ginger
1/2 teaspoon cinnamon
1/2 teaspoon nutmeg
20 chopped walnut halves
zest of 1/2 an orange
2 cups flour
4 teaspoons baking powder
60 grams butter, melted
2 eggs
1 cup milk
1/2 teaspoon vanilla essence
4 tablespoons honey

nutty topping
2 tablespoons chopped walnuts
1 tablespoon soft brown sugar

1. Preheat oven to 200°C. Lightly grease 12 muffin tins.
2. In a bowl combine the chopped prunes, sugar, cloves, ginger, cinnamon, nutmeg, walnuts and orange zest.
3. Sift together flour and baking powder into a bowl and make a well in the centre.
4. In another bowl lightly whisk together the melted butter, eggs, milk, vanilla essence and honey, and pour over prune mixture.
5. Fold prune mixture into dry ingredients and stir quickly to combine.
6. Spoon mixture into prepared muffin tins.
7. To make the nutty topping, mix together walnuts and sugar

and lightly sprinkle on top of each muffin.
8. Bake for 12–15 minutes or until muffins spring back when lightly pressed.

Makes 12

rhubarb and custard muffins

2 cups flour
2 teaspoons baking powder
1 teaspoon baking soda
1 1/2 cups raw rhubarb, finely sliced
1/2 cup soft brown sugar
60 grams butter, melted
1 teaspoon vanilla essence
1 cup buttermilk
1 egg
3/4 cup prepared custard

1. Preheat oven to 220°C. Lightly grease 12 muffin tins.
2. Sift together flour, baking powder and baking soda into a bowl and make a well in the centre.
3. Place rhubarb in another bowl and coat with the sugar.
4. In another bowl whisk together the melted butter, vanilla essence, buttermilk and egg. Stir in the rhubarb and sugar.
5. Fold egg mixture into dry ingredients and stir quickly to combine.
6. Spoon mixture into prepared muffin tins.
7. Using the back of a small spoon, make an indent in the centre of the muffin and spoon in one tablespoon of prepared custard.
8. Bake for 12–15 minutes or until muffins spring back when lightly pressed.

Makes 12

maple fruit and mixed nut muffins

100 grams pitted dates, chopped
$1/4$ cup maple syrup
$1/4$ cup soft brown sugar
60 grams butter
1 cup boiling water
1 teaspoon baking soda
2 ripe bananas, roughly chopped
$1/4$ cup walnuts, chopped
$1/4$ cup almonds, chopped
$1/4$ cup pistachios, chopped
2 cups flour
3 teaspoons baking powder
1 teaspoon cinnamon
$1/2$ teaspoon ground cardamom
maple syrup to drizzle on top

1. Preheat oven to 200°C. Lightly grease 12 muffin tins.
2. Place dates, maple syrup, sugar, butter, boiling water and baking soda in a bowl and stir to combine. When cool, stir in the chopped bananas, walnuts, almonds and pistachio nuts.
3. Sift together flour, baking powder, cinnamon and ground cardamom into a bowl and make a well in the centre.
4. Fold the banana mixture into the dry ingredients and stir quickly to combine.
5. Spoon mixture into prepared muffin tins and bake for 12–15 minutes or until muffins spring back when lightly pressed.
6. Serve warm drizzled with maple syrup.

Makes 12

carrot, mixed fruit and bran muffins

1 cup flour
3 teaspoons baking powder
1 teaspoon baking soda
1 teaspoon cinnamon
pinch of salt
1 cup bran cereal (I use the bran that looks like twigs)
$1/2$ cup sugar
2 tablespoons desiccated coconut
1 egg
1 cup milk
1 teaspoon vanilla essence
1 cup grated carrot
1 cup stewed or canned apple
$1/2$ cup raisins
8 chopped dates

1. Preheat oven to 200°C. Lightly grease 12 muffin tins.
2. Sift together flour, baking powder, baking soda, cinnamon and salt into a bowl.
3. Stir in bran cereal, sugar and coconut, and make a well in the centre.
4. In another bowl lightly whisk together egg, milk and vanilla essence.
5. Stir in grated carrot, stewed apple, raisins and dates.
6. Fold apple mixture into dry ingredients and stir quickly to combine.
7. Spoon mixture into prepared muffin tins and bake for 12–15 minutes or until muffins spring back when lightly pressed.

Makes 12

marbled chocolate and orange muffins with sour cream icing

2 cups flour
4 teaspoons baking powder
$\frac{1}{2}$ cup ground almonds
$\frac{1}{2}$ cup sugar
2 eggs
60 grams butter, melted
$\frac{1}{2}$ cup fresh orange juice
$\frac{1}{2}$ cup milk
20 milk chocolate buttons, melted in a basin over boiling water

sour cream icing
6 tablespoons icing sugar
1 tablespoon cocoa
3 tablespoons sour cream
1 teaspoon butter, softened
hot water to mix

1. Preheat oven to 200°C. Lightly grease 12 muffin tins.
2. Sift together flour, baking powder and ground almonds into a bowl, stir in sugar and make a well in the centre.
3. Whisk together the eggs, melted butter, orange juice and milk.
4. Fold egg mixture into dry ingredients and stir quickly to combine.
5. Divide muffin mixture into two bowls.
6. Fold melted chocolate into one bowl of the muffin mixture and stir to combine.
7. Gently swirl this chocolate mixture through plain mixture to create a marble effect. Do not overstir or you will lose the marbling.
8. Carefully spoon mixture into prepared muffin tins and bake for 12–15 minutes or until muffins spring back when lightly pressed. Allow to cool.
9. To make sour cream icing, mix icing sugar, cocoa, sour cream, softened butter and enough water in a bowl. Spread over muffins.

Makes 12

dusted chocolate muffins

60 grams butter
1 tablespoon golden syrup
$^1/_2$ cup milk
1 teaspoon baking soda
1$^1/_2$ cups flour
1 teaspoon baking powder
3 teaspoons cocoa
$^3/_4$ cup sugar
$^1/_2$ cup extra milk
icing sugar to dust top

1. Preheat oven to 200°C. Lightly grease 10 muffin tins.
2. Place butter, golden syrup and milk in a pot and gently heat until butter melts. Stir in baking soda and allow to cool slightly.
3. Sift together flour, baking powder and cocoa into a bowl, stir in sugar and make a well in the centre.
4. Fold butter mixture into dry ingredients, add extra half cup of milk and stir quickly to combine.
5. Spoon mixture into prepared muffin tins and bake for 12–15 minutes or until muffins spring back when lightly pressed.
6. Serve dusted with icing sugar.

Makes 8–10

just desserts

a little figgy and lime marmalade pudding muffins served with kahlua cream

12 dried figs, chopped
1/4 cup lime marmalade
1/4 cup soft brown sugar
60 grams butter
1/4 cup water
1 teaspoon baking soda
2 eggs
3/4 cup milk
2 cups flour
3 teaspoons baking powder
1/2 teaspoon mixed spice

kahlua cream
1/4 cup whipped cream
1 tablespoon kahlua liqueur (or liqueur of your choice)

1. Preheat oven to 200°C. Lightly grease 12 muffin tins.
2. Place chopped figs, lime marmalade, sugar, butter and water in a pot and gently heat until butter melts. Remove from heat and stir in baking soda.
3. In a bowl lightly whisk together the eggs and milk, and stir into cooled fig mixture.
4. Sift together flour, baking powder and mixed spice into a bowl and make a well in the centre.
5. Fold fig mixture into dry ingredients and stir quickly to combine.
6. Spoon mixture into prepared muffin tins and bake for 12–15 minutes or until muffins spring back when lightly pressed.
7. To make kahlua cream, stir kahlua liqueur into whipped cream. Serve muffins topped with one teaspoon of kahlua cream.

Makes 12

a peach trifle of muffins

6 maderia muffins (page 97) or muffin of your choice
1/4 cup strawberry jam
1/4 cup sweet sherry or gingerale
1 x 400 gram can peach slices, drained (reserve 2 tablespoons syrup)
3 tablespoons custard powder
2 cups milk
3 tablespoons sugar
1/2 cup whipped cream
1/4 cup chopped walnuts

1. Slice muffins into 2cm rounds and spread with strawberry jam.
2. Arrange slices over the base and sides of a glass serving bowl, reserving some for the top.
3. Mix together the sherry and peach syrup and drizzle over the muffins.
4. Cover muffin slices with drained peach slices and top with remaining muffin slices.
5. Place custard powder in a small jug and add enough milk to form a smooth paste.
6. In a pot gently heat the remaining milk and sugar, and when warm stir in the mixed custard powder. Stir on a low heat until custard thickens. Remove from heat and allow to cool.
7. Spoon cooled custard over muffins and peaches. Spread custard with whipped cream and decorate with chopped walnuts.

Serves 6

sticky date muffins drizzled with golden syrup cream

1 1/2 cups dates, chopped
1/2 cup orange juice
zest of 1 orange (reserve some for the top)
1/2 cup soft brown sugar
50 grams butter
2 1/2 cups flour
4 teaspoons baking powder
1 teaspoon baking soda
1 teaspoon mixed spice
1 cup buttermilk
1 egg

golden syrup cream
1 tablespoon golden syrup
3/4 cup whipped cream

1. Place dates and orange juice in a pot and gently bring to the boil. Simmer for a couple of minutes on a low heat, then add the orange zest, sugar and butter. Remove from the heat and stir to combine all the ingredients until the butter has melted. Allow to cool.

2. Preheat oven to 200°C. Lightly grease 12 muffin tins.

3. Sift together flour, baking powder, baking soda and mixed spice into a bowl and make a well in the centre.

4. In another bowl lightly whisk together the buttermilk and egg. Pour over the date mixture.

5. Fold date mixture into the dry ingredients and stir quickly to combine.

6. Spoon mixture into prepared muffin tins. Sprinkle with remaining orange zest. Bake for 12–15 minutes or until muffins spring back when lightly pressed.

7. To make golden syrup cream, streak golden syrup lightly through the whipped cream and spoon one tablespoon on top of each muffin.

Makes 12

muffin and butter pudding with a whisky custard

½ cup raisins
8 prunes, chopped
1 tablespoon whisky
6 muffins of your choice, fresh or stale
30 grams butter, softened

whisky custard
2 eggs
¼ cup sugar
1½ cups milk
1 teaspoon vanilla essence
2 tablespoons whisky
½ teaspoon cinnamon
½ teaspoon nutmeg

1. Place raisins and prunes in a bowl and sprinkle with one tablespoon of whisky. Cover and leave to soak for 30 minutes.
2. Preheat oven to 180°C and lightly grease a medium-sized shallow ovenproof dish.
3. Slice each muffin into three rounds, spread with softened butter and overlap half the rounds on the bottom of the dish.
4. Sprinkle the muffin layer with the whisky-soaked fruit and cover with the remaining muffin slices.
5. To make whisky custard, whisk together the eggs, sugar, milk, vanilla essence, whisky, cinnamon and nutmeg in a bowl.
6. Pour custard mixture over the muffins and bake for 30–35 minutes or until pudding is set and lightly browned.

Serves 4–6
Note: This is a great way to use up muffins stored in the freezer or stale muffins.

tahitian lime meringue muffins

meringue
1 egg white
³/₄ cup sugar
2 tablespoons boiling water
1 teaspoon vinegar
1 teaspoon baking powder

muffins
2 cups flour
4 teaspoons baking powder
¹/₂ cup ground almonds
¹/₂ cup sugar
60 grams butter, melted

2 eggs
zest of ¹/₂ a lime
1 cup milk
6 tablespoons lime curd (refer page 151)

1. Preheat oven to 180°C. Lightly grease 12 muffin tins.
2. To make meringue, cover egg white with sugar and vinegar, add boiling water and beat until very stiff, then beat in baking powder.
3. Sift together flour and baking powder into a bowl. Stir in ground almonds and sugar, and make a well in the centre.
4. In another bowl lightly whisk together melted butter, eggs, lime zest and milk.
5. Fold egg mixture into dry ingredients and stir quickly to combine.
6. Spoon mixture into prepared muffin tins. Use the back of the spoon to form a small indent in the top each muffin and fill with one and a half teaspoons of lime curd.
7. Cover top of each muffin with meringue and bake for 14–16 minutes or until muffins spring back when lightly pressed. Allow muffins to cool for 10 minutes before carefully removing to a cake rack.

Makes 12

sort of a nutty baklava muffin with orange syrup

nutty baklava filling
4 tablespoons chopped walnuts
2 tablespoons chopped pecans
2 tablespoons chopped pistachios
1 tablespoon maple syrup
1 teaspoon ground cinnamon
8 chopped fresh dates

muffin mixture
2 cups flour
4 teaspoons baking powder
1/4 cup soft brown sugar
60 grams butter, melted
1 egg
1 cup milk

orange syrup topping
3 tablespoons maple syrup
1/2 teaspoon cinnamon
pinch of ground cloves
1/4 cup fresh orange juice
2 teaspoons grated orange zest

1. Preheat oven to 200°C. Lightly grease 12 muffin tins.
2. To make filling, combine the walnuts, pecans, pistachios, maple syrup, cinnamon and dates in a bowl.
3. To make muffins, sift together flour and baking powder into a bowl, stir in sugar and make a well in the centre.
4. In another bowl lightly whisk together the melted butter, egg and milk.
5. Fold egg mixture into dry ingredients and stir quickly to combine.

6. Spoon one tablespoon of mixture into each muffin tin. Sprinkle with nutty baklava filling and top with remaining muffin mixture. Sprinkle the remaining filling over the top of each muffin.

7. Bake for 12–15 minutes or until muffins spring back when lightly pressed.

8. While muffins are cooking prepare the orange syrup topping. In a small pot heat together the maple syrup, cinnamon, cloves, orange juice and orange zest. Simmer on a low heat for 5–8 minutes to thicken and reduce.

9. Allow muffins to cool in tins for 5 minutes before removing to a cake rack.

10. Spoon syrup over the top of the muffins and serve while still warm.

Makes 12

boysenberry and lemon muffins with a crumble topping

2 cups flour
4 teaspoons baking powder
1/4 teaspoon ground nutmeg
pinch of salt
2 cups boysenberries
3/4 cup sugar
1 tablespoon lemon zest
juice of 1/2 a lemon
60 grams butter, melted
1 egg
3/4 cup milk

crumble topping
1/4 cup flour
1/4 cup sugar
15 grams butter
icing sugar to dust top

1. Preheat oven to 200°C. Lightly grease 12 muffin tins.
2. Sift together flour, baking powder, nutmeg and salt into a bowl and make a well in the centre.
3. Place boysenberries in another bowl and cover with the sugar.
4. In another bowl whisk together the lemon zest, juice, melted butter, egg and milk. Pour over the boysenberry mixture.
5. Fold the boysenberry mixture into dry ingredients and stir quickly to combine.
6. Spoon mixture into prepared muffin tins.
7. To make the crumble topping, rub together the flour, sugar and butter in

a small bowl. Sprinkle over the top of each muffin.

8. Bake for 12–15 minutes or until the muffins spring back when lightly pressed. Allow muffins to cool for a few minutes in the tin before removing to a cake rack.

9. Serve lightly dusted with icing sugar.

Makes 12

upside-down pineapple muffins

6 teaspoons golden syrup
6 pineapple rings, canned in natural juice, drained (reserve ¼ cup juice)
1 cup flour
2 teaspoons baking powder
¼ cup sugar
30 grams butter, melted
1 egg
¼ cup pineapple juice
2 tablespoons milk
½ teaspoon vanilla essence

1. Preheat oven to 200°C. Lightly grease 6 muffin tins.
2. Place one teaspoon golden syrup into each muffin tin and top with a pineapple ring. You may need to cut a small wedge out of each ring to make it fit in the tin.
3. Sift together flour and baking powder into a bowl, stir in sugar and make a well in the centre.
4. In another bowl lightly whisk together the melted butter, eggs, pineapple juice, milk and vanilla essence.
5. Fold egg mixture into dry ingredients and stir quickly to combine.
6. Spoon mixture on top of pineapple ring and bake for 12–15 minutes or until muffins spring back when lightly pressed.

Makes 6

Just a thought:
I like to serve this pudding warm with a little extra drizzle of golden syrup and a dab of whipped cream. You could try other fruits such as apple or peaches.

special occasions

brandied fruit muffins

3 cups mixed dried fruit
1/4 cup brandy
1 cup orange juice
1 cup flour
2 teaspoons baking powder
1/2 teaspoon mixed spice
1/2 teaspoon cinnamon
1/2 teaspoon nutmeg
2 tablespoons soft brown sugar
red and green glacé cherries and mixed nuts for decorating top (optional)

1. In a bowl combine the mixed fruit, brandy and orange juice, cover and leave to soak overnight.
2. Preheat oven to 180°C. Lightly grease 12 muffin tins.
3. Sift together flour, baking powder, mixed spice, cinnamon and nutmeg into a bowl, stir in sugar and make a well in the centre.
4. Fold soaked mixed fruit into dry ingredients and stir quickly to combine.
5. Spoon mixture into prepared muffin tins and decorate with cherries and nuts. Bake for 15–20 minutes or until muffins spring back when lightly pressed.

Makes 12

christmas fruit mince muffins

fruit mince
2 apples, peeled and grated
$1/2$ cup mixed dried fruit
1 teaspoon grated lemon zest
juice of 1 lemon
1 teaspoon cinnamon
1 teaspoon mixed spice
$1/2$ teaspoon nutmeg

muffin mixture
2 cups flour
4 teaspoons baking powder
$1/2$ cup sugar
60 grams butter, melted
$3/4$ cup milk
2 eggs
icing sugar to dust on top

1. To make Christmas fruit mince, mix together the apple, mixed fruit, lemon zest, juice, cinnamon, mixed spice and nutmeg.
2. Preheat oven to 200°C. Lightly grease 12 muffin tins.
3. Sift together flour, baking powder and sugar into a bowl and make a well in the centre.
4. In another bowl lightly whisk together the melted butter, milk and eggs, then pour over the mince.
5. Fold fruit mince mixture into dry ingredients and stir quickly to combine.
6. Spoon mixture into prepared muffin tins and bake for 12–15 minutes or until muffins spring back when lightly pressed.
7. Allow muffins to cool before dusting with icing sugar.

Makes 12

berry white christmas muffins

250 grams frozen raspberries (reserve 12 raspberries for the top)
1/2 cup sugar
2 cups flour
4 teaspoons baking powder
60 grams butter, melted
2 eggs
1 cup milk
120 grams white chocolate melts, chopped
icing sugar to dust

1. Preheat oven to 200°C. Lightly grease 12 muffin tins.
2. Place raspberries in a bowl, sprinkle with sugar and allow to thaw for 5 minutes.
3. Sift together flour and baking powder into a bowl and make a well in the centre.
4. In another bowl lightly whisk together the melted butter, eggs and milk. Stir in raspberries and white chocolate.
5. Fold the raspberry mixture into the dry ingredients and stir quickly to combine.
6. Spoon mixture into prepared muffin tins and top each muffin with a reserved raspberry.
7. Bake for 12–15 minutes or until muffins spring back when lightly pressed.
8. Allow muffins to cool for a few minutes before removing from tin and dusting with icing sugar.

Makes 12

hidden easter egg muffins

$1^1/_2$ cups flour
$^1/_2$ cup custard powder
4 teaspoons baking powder
1 teaspoon cinnamon
$^1/_2$ cup sugar
60 grams butter, melted
2 eggs
1 cup milk
12 very small cream caramel Easter eggs (foil removed!)
icing sugar to dust

1. Preheat oven to 200°C. Lightly grease 12 muffin tins.
2. Sift together the flour, custard powder, baking powder, cinnamon and
   sugar into a bowl and make a well in the centre.
3. In another bowl lightly whisk together the melted butter, eggs and milk.
4. Fold egg mixture into dry ingredients and quickly stir to combine.
5. Spoon one tablespoon of muffin mixture into each prepared tin.
   Place one caramel Easter egg in the centre of each and cover with the
   remaining mixture.
6. Bake for 12–15 minutes or until muffins spring back when lightly pressed.
7. Dust with icing sugar before serving.

Makes 12

spiced easter muffins with a cross of lemon icing

2 cups flour
3 teaspoons baking powder
$1/2$ teaspoon baking soda
2 teaspoons mixed spice
$1/2$ cup soft brown sugar
60 grams butter, melted
2 eggs
1 cup milk
2 cups mixed dried fruit
icing sugar for dusting

lemon icing
$1/2$ cup icing sugar
2 teaspoons butter, softened
lemon juice to mix

1. Preheat oven to 200°C. Lightly grease 12 muffin tins.
2. Sift together flour, baking powder, baking soda and mixed spice into a bowl, stir in sugar and make a well in the centre.
3. In another bowl lightly whisk together the melted butter, eggs and milk and stir in the dried fruit.
4. Fold dried fruit mixture into dry ingredients and stir quickly to combine.
5. Spoon mixture into prepared muffin tins and bake for 12–15 minutes or until muffins spring back when lightly pressed.
6. To make lemon icing, mix together the icing sugar and butter, and add sufficient lemon juice to make an icing of spreading consistency.
7. Allow muffins to cool, dust with icing sugar and drizzle a lemon icing cross on top.

Makes 12

goody gum drop party muffins

2¼ cups flour
4 teaspoons baking powder
¾ cup sugar
140 grams wine gums (reserve 12 for top and cut the rest in half)
60 grams butter, melted
2 eggs
¾ cup milk

1. Preheat oven to 200°C. Lightly grease 12 muffin tins.
2. Sift together flour, baking powder and sugar into a bowl and make a well in the centre.
3. Stir in wine gums.
4. In another bowl lightly whisk together the melted butter, eggs and milk. Pour into dry ingredients and stir quickly to combine.
5. Spoon mixture into prepared muffin tins, top each muffin with a wine gum and bake for 12–15 minutes or until muffins spring back when lightly pressed.

Makes 12

children's birthday hundreds and thousands mini muffins with pink icing

2 cups flour
3 teaspoons baking powder
1 teaspoon baking soda
$1/2$ cup sugar
4 tablespoons hundreds and thousands
1 teaspoon vanilla essence
50 grams butter, melted
1 cup buttermilk
2 eggs

pink icing

1 cup icing sugar
2 teaspoons butter, softened
1 small drop red food colouring

hot water to mix
4 tablespoons hundreds and thousands
  for topping

1. Preheat oven to 200°C. Lightly grease 24 mini muffin tins.
2. Sift together flour, baking powder and baking soda into a bowl, stir in sugar and hundreds and thousands, and make a well in the centre.
3. In another bowl lightly whisk together vanilla essence, melted butter, buttermilk and eggs.
4. Fold egg mixture into dry ingredients and stir quickly to combine.
5. Spoon mixture into 24 prepared mini muffin tins and bake for 10–13 minutes or until muffins spring back when lightly pressed.
6. To make pink icing, mix together icing sugar, softened butter and small drop of red food colouring with sufficient hot water to make a spreadable icing.
7. Lightly ice top of each muffin. Spread hundreds and thousands on a plate and gently dip the iced muffin into mixture to lightly coat.

Makes 24

black russian cocktail mini muffins

2 cups flour
4 teaspoons baking powder
1/4 teaspoon salt
200 grams smoked salmon, cut into small pieces
juice and zest of 1 lime
freshly ground black pepper
1 cup milk
60 grams butter, melted
2 eggs, beaten
4 tablespoons finely chopped chives

caviar garnish
8 tablespoons sour cream
4 tablespoons black caviar

1. Preheat oven to 200°C. Lightly grease 24 mini muffin tins.
2. Sift together the flour, baking powder and salt into a bowl and make a well in the centre.
3. Place smoked salmon in another small bowl and cover with lime juice, zest and black pepper.
4. In another bowl lightly whisk together the milk, melted butter and eggs. Stir in the smoked salmon and chives.
5. Fold salmon mixture into dry ingredients and stir quickly to combine.
6. Spoon mixture into 24 prepared mini muffin tins and bake for 10–13 minutes or until muffins spring back when lightly pressed.
7. Allow muffins to cool. Slice the top off each muffin and dab top of muffin with one teaspoon of sour cream and half a teaspoon of black caviar. Place the lid back at an angle.

Makes 24 mini muffins

home-made and in
the pantry

aunty hilda's apricot jam

500 grams dried apricots, roughly chopped
5 cups water
5 cups sugar

1. Place apricots in a large bowl, cover with water and leave to soak overnight.
2. Drain liquid into large pot and bring to the boil.
3. Remove from heat and stir in sugar, then bring to the boil again.
4. Add apricots and boil rapidly for 30 minutes, stirring occasionally.
5. To test, place a small spoonful of jam on a cold saucer and leave to cool for a minute. When it gels the jam is ready.
6. Pour jam into hot sterilised jars and seal while hot.

strawberry conserve

2 chips fresh strawberries, washed and hulled
4 cups sugar

1. Place strawberries in a large pot, cover with sugar and leave to stand overnight.
2. Place pot on a low heat and gently bring to the boil.
3. Boil rapidly for 30 minutes, stirring occasionally.
4. Pour conserve into hot sterilised jars and seal while hot.

lime or lemon curd

80 grams butter (unsalted is best)
1/2 cup lime or lemon juice
2 teaspoons grated lime or lemon zest
1/2 cup sugar
3 eggs, lightly beaten

1. Place butter in a pot and melt on a low heat. Do not allow to burn.
2. Remove pot from heat and lightly whisk in the lime/lemon juice, zest, sugar and beaten eggs.
3. Cook on a low heat, whisking until curd is smooth and thick and coats the back of a spoon.
4. Pour lime or lemon curd into hot sterilised jars and seal when cold.

Makes approximately 1 1/4 cups

tomato salsa

1 small red onion, finely chopped
4 firm tomatoes, chopped into small pieces
2 cloves garlic, crushed
1 teaspoon sweet chilli sauce
1/2 teaspoon salt
freshly ground black pepper

1. In a bowl combine all the ingredients and chill until ready to use.

ginger marmalade

2 large or 3 small grapefruit
1 lemon
2 litres water
1 kilo sugar
50 grams preserved ginger, cut small

Preparation for making marmalade starts the night before.

1. Slice grapefruit and lemon very finely, remove pips and place in non-metallic basin.
2. Cover with water and leave to soak overnight.
3. The following day, add fruit ingredients to a large pot, bring to the boil and continue boiling for 20 minutes.
4. Gently pour the sugar into the fruit mixture and bring slowly back to the boil. Add chopped ginger and continue boiling for a further 30 minutes.
5. Test for setting by placing a teaspoonful of marmalade on a cold saucer and allow to cool. When it gels the marmalade is ready.
6. Allow to stand for 5 minutes before pouring into hot sterilised jars and seal while hot.

spicy tomato and apple chutney

1 kilo tomatoes, chopped into small chunks
700 grams green apples, e.g. Granny Smith, thinly sliced
3 onions, finely chopped
2$1/4$ cups vinegar
50 grams salt
$1/2$ teaspoon pepper
1 teaspoon cloves
1 fresh chilli, deseeded and finely chopped
450 grams soft brown sugar
225 grams seedless raisins
100 grams lemon zest, finely sliced
juice of 1 lemon

1. Place tomatoes, apples and onions in a large pot.
2. Pour in the vinegar and add the salt, pepper, cloves, chilli, sugar, raisins and lemon zest.
3. Bring to the boil stirring all the time and then simmer gently for 3 hours. Stir occasionally to prevent sticking.
4. Add lemon juice during cooking time.
5. To test, trail wooden spoon across top of mixture. If trail fills with liquid then the chutney is not ready. Keep simmering and test again.
6. When ready allow chutney to cool for 5 minutes before spooning into hot sterilised jars.
7. Seal when cold.

buttering up

lime chilli butter

60 grams butter, softened
1 small red chilli (remove seeds) finely chopped
    or 1/4 teaspoon chilli powder
juice and zest of 1/2 a lime
pinch of salt

1. Use a fork to mash all ingredients together in a bowl.
   Chill until ready to use.

parsley butter

60 grams butter, softened
2 tablespoons parsley, finely chopped
1 clove garlic, crushed

1. Use a fork to mash all the ingredients together in a bowl.
   Chill until ready to use.

honeycomb butter

60 grams butter, softened
4 tablespoons honeycomb

1. Use a fork to mash the butter and honeycomb together.
   Chill until ready to use.

vanilla sugar

1 kilo white sugar
3 vanilla pods

1. Fill an airtight container with sugar.
2. Cut the vanilla pods in half and press into the sugar.
3. Leave for at least 2 weeks before using.

Note: Vanilla sugar will keep indefinitely in an airtight container, and you can top it up from time to time with more sugar.

basil pesto

1/2 bunch or 1 cup fresh basil
1/2 cup parsley, chopped
50 grams pine nuts
3 cloves garlic
70 grams Parmesan cheese, grated
1/2 cup olive oil

1. Place all ingredients in a food processor and blend until smooth.
2. Pour into a jar and store in the refrigerator. It will keep for about
   2 weeks.

Did you know ...

Baking powder
is made up of baking soda (bicarbonate of soda), cream of tartar and cornstarch. It contains both acid and alkaline components so does not need to be used with an acidic ingredient such as buttermilk.

Baking soda
(also known as bicarbonate of soda) is an alkaline raising agent and is best used with buttermilk, yoghurt, lemon or sour cream.

Buttermilk
is a cultured milk which, when used in baking, produces a lighter mixture. Buttermilk is readily available in many supermarkets, but you can make your own by adding 1 teaspoon of vinegar to 1 cup of regular milk. Leave it to stand for a few minutes to allow the milk to curdle.

Chorizo sausage
is a Spanish sausage made from smoked, coarsely ground pork spiced with garlic and paprika. It is available in the deli section of supermarkets and can be bought in hot or medium-hot varieties – ask at the counter. And, yes, you can buy just one.

Cornmeal
is also known as polenta and is a finely milled maize flour.

Feta cheese
originated in Greece and is a white, crumbly cheese traditionally made from goats' milk, but now more often you will find it made from cows' milk.

Goats' cheese
is a soft, moist cheese also referred to as chèvre, which is – surprise – French for cheese made with goats' milk.

Mascarpone
is a fresh, unripened soft double or triple cream cheese very much like clotted cream. Culture is added to the cream of pure cow's milk then allowed to mature and thicken. It is often used as a dessert cream.

Mixed spice and allspice
are not the same. Mixed spice, as the name suggests, is a combination of cloves, ginger, nutmeg, allspice and cinnamon. Allspice, also known as pimento or Jamaica pepper, is the dried berry from a tropical Central American tree.

Mozzarella
is a moist, stretched, curd cheese – great served with tomatoes. Also used in pizza-type recipes.

Pastrami
is a cured, spiced beef coated with black pepper and chilli.

Prosciutto
is an Italian smoked ham from the hind leg of a pig and is also known as Parma ham. It is usually sliced paper-thin and can be bought at most supermarkets and delis.

Ricotta
is a low-fat cheese made from the whey of milk rather than the curd.

Roasted peppers
are very easy to prepare by placing them under a hot grill or in a hot oven until the skin blackens and blisters. Place them in a plastic bag to sweat and when cool enough to handle peel off the blackened skin, de-seed and cut into strips. Delicious in salads, sandwiches, scrambled eggs and, of course, muffins.

Rhubarb
is a vegetable not a fruit, and the leaves are poisonous. When preparing rhubarb stalks for cooking, leave the strings on as this will help prevent the rhubarb becoming mushy and losing colour.

Index